THE SPARROW'S SPIRIT

*A Champion Wrestler's Lifetime Reflections
on Prayer and Perseverance*

Bill Welker

To: Coach Dick Edge
I still remember
wrestling in the motel room
at Nitro in 1972! I also
remember how hot and cramped
the HS was! What a
state tournament!
Billy W
7-7-18

RoseDog 🐾 Books
PITTSBURGH, PENNSYLVANIA 15238

RoseDog Books
585 Alpha Drive
Suite 103
Pittsburgh, PA 15238
Visit our website at *www.rosedogbookstore.com*

ISBN: 978-1-4809-6671-0
eISBN: 978-1-4809-6694-9

The Sparrow's Spirit is dedicated to all the students that I have taught and coached for 40 years. They were the inspiration for all my professional endeavors to develop their minds and bodies. I have always believed in the following quote:

> *"He who is only an athlete is too crude, too vulgar, too much a savage. He who is a scholar only is too soft. The ideal citizen is the scholar-athlete, a man of thought and a man of action."*
>
> - Plato

It is also dedicated to my wife, Peggy, who has supported me throughout our entire lives together. Her encouragement has been my source of strength during difficult times.

And finally, I dedicate my memoirs to our parents, William and Dorothy Welker & Howard and Margaret Bainbridge, who taught Peggy and me to believe in ourselves and to thank God for all his blessings.

• • •

CONTENTS

Acknowledgments

A special thank-you to the late Coach Joseph J. Thomas and the late Sgt. Mark J. Gerrity, USMC, men who demonstrated the highest ideals of sincere friendship.

I also want to thank Human Kinetics staff members Jason Muzinic, Bill Johnson and Jennifer Mulcahey for their assistance in producing these memoirs. Human Kinetics was the publisher of my former works.

A very special note of appreciation to my developmental editor is forwarded to Melissa Wuske for her invaluable advice during the revision stage of the book.

I deeply thank Tom Elling for his expertise in proofreading the manuscript.

I would be remiss if I didn't mention those individuals who influenced my life. Besides my two role models – Dad and Coach Mal Paul, there were Coach Lyman "Beans" Weaver, Glenn Flegal, Lynn Holderman, Ron Mauck, Bill McEldowney, Bill Hinegardner, Dick Edge, Dr. Vince Monseau, Larry Ritchie, Mary Kay Reisinger, Andy Garber, Woody Yoder, George Kovalick, Bobby Douglas, Bill Archer, Larry Deaton, Joe Handlan, Ray Marling, Jim Monderine, Ray Chenoweth, Sam Defillippo, Pat Walling, Thea and John Gompers, Joey and Abbey Maroon, Barry Gashel, Rod Oldham, Ken McWilliams, Chris Diserio, Mike Stalnaker, Bert Shelek, Dave Adams, Bob Fehrs, Eric Carder, Jack Regis, Dr. Marilyn Fairbanks, Dr. Steven Stahl, Ellery Newberry, Claude Readly, the Peery Family, Dr. Steven Rinehart, Bill Van Horne, Nick Bedway, Adam Townsend, Don Clegg, Mike Myer, Seth Staskey, and Bubba Kapral.

— Dr. Bill Welker

PROLOGUE

"Mrs. Welker, your son Billy is a piece of work."

Those words of my elementary principal, Mr. Newberry, were spoken after I'd run panic-stricken home from school in the spring of 1954. I'd gotten into trouble at school that day and was running away from Mr. Newberry: He was about to paddle me — again — for misbehaving.

I told my parents that I'd misbehaved in my first grade reading class and the principal was going to punish me at the end of the day. I tried to make excuses for my behavior, but in the end, my father sent me immediately to bed.

The next day my mother took me to the principal's office and instructed me to apologize to Mr. Newberry. In tears, I remorsefully pleaded for forgiveness, begging not to be paddled.

The principal accepted my apology. But he made it clear that if I misbehaved again I would have to face the consequences of my actions.

My mother thanked the principal for his understanding and pledged to work with me regarding discipline in school.

Then he issued his humorous declaration.

• • •

Certainly, Principal Newberry was right: I am a bit different.

My life, as told in the pages of this book, tells the story of my humorous, good-natured, and my many outright stupid actions growing up. But, more than that, no matter my life stage, the undercurrent of what I've done and who I am is my parents — the way they raised me, and the way my mother prayed on my behalf.

CHAPTER ONE

My Elementary Years

"Success covers a multitude of Blunders."
                                    - George Bernard Shaw

I grew up in the anthracite coal region of Pennsylvania in a small town, Shamokin. One of its claims to fame is that Shamokin has the largest man-made coal bank in the world, which was burning underground. On rainy days, I could see the smoke rising.

Most notably, Thomas Edison briefly lived in the area and established the Edison Illuminating Company in Shamokin the fall of 1882. In fact, Shamokin's St. Edward's Catholic Church was one of the first churches in the world to be furnished with electric lighting by Edison on September 22, 1883.

Shamokin was also the hometown of Stanley A. Coveleski. A major league pitcher, he was inducted into the Baseball Hall of Fame in 1969. Stan passed away in 1984 at the venerable age of 94.

I have always loved the people that populated my hometown. From all socio-economic classes and nationalities, they taught me so much about life during my 18 years as a youth growing up in Shamokin.

• • •

I attended Washington Elementary School, a small neighborhood school just a block away from our house. The best part of the day was my 45-minute lunch break at home. Mom would usually prepare grilled ham and cheese sandwiches, accompanied with chocolate milk or Ovaltine.

While eating I would watch the *Lunch with Soupy Sales Show*. I'll never forget the time Soupy Sales told all the kids to send him the green bills in their mother's purses. He even gave an address.

I never sent any money, but other kids around the country did. To the best of my knowledge, Soupy Sales received 100s of dollars with no return addresses.

Although he gave the money to charity, his show was off the air for two weeks. I loved the show and couldn't wait until Soupy Sales was back on the network.

When I was older, I learned that Soupy's novel sense of humor throughout the years got him into trouble more than once with the FCC, especially the time he said, "Why is it every time I see F, you see K?"

As kids, we never picked up on his adult undertones. We just loved his funny routines on the boob tube.

Later in his life when Soupy Sales was being interviewed, he related the hilarious prank his crew played on him. Soupy Sales had a door he opened where a hand or large hairy paw would reach out and pat him all over his face. Often it was a television or movie celebrity.

Well, one time when Soupy opened the door, he witnessed a topless young lady dancing in front of him. It was also on the TV monitor backstage. Soupy was sure his television career was over.

Soupy's shows always ended with a pie in his face.

I just had to tell about my super lunches with Soupy. He always fired me up for my afternoon escapades at school.

· · ·

Let me tell you, my elementary years were far from being uneventful. I was a scamp who did some very foolish things. My brother, Floyd, who was five years older, was not as irksome, but close. We kept our teachers busy those early formative years.

I also had serious reading problems in elementary school. Simply said, I spent so much time concentrating on "phonics" to pronounce the words that I was unable to comprehend the material read. I gradually grow out of it.

As a first and second grader, it seemed that I might have future discipline problems as a student. Miss Evans, my first grade teacher, was not impressed with my talkative spirit in class. And I know that for a fact because my mom kept my first grade report card.

There is a section on the report card which was designated "Your child shows undesirable habits as checked." One area to be checked was "Annoys others talking." Miss Evans crossed out 'others' and replaced it with "Annoys ME talking."

Years later, I asked my mother, "Why did you keep this report card?"

She said, trying not to hurt my feelings, "Well, Billy, it was one of your best report cards in elementary school."

It was all C's and D's.

Ouch.

.   .   .

In the spring of my second grade year, my neighborhood friends and I were being bullied by a big seventh grader. My brother, Floyd, observed it and came to our aid, telling the tormentor to knock it off.

This bully completely ignored Floyd's admonishment, studying one who looked into his chest while talking.

A mistake!

Floyd and this juvenile fought, fist-to-cuff, in front of my buddies and me for more than half an hour. When it was over, no one won, but the boy walked away and never bothered us again.

Although Floyd always teased me, he wasn't going to let anybody else pick on his little "bro."

.   .   .

In third grade, I had a cap gun that I really liked. I broke it in the school yard one Saturday morning. I was so upset and devised a plan to acquire a new one, even though I didn't have any money.

I bought the gun at a local F. W. Woolworth store. I went into the establishment and walked right up to the cap gun display. Looking around to make sure that no one could see me, I took a new gun from the counter, replaced it with my broken gun and walked out of the store undetected.

Upon returning to the school yard, my conscious started to bother me. My parents didn't raise their two boys to steal.

What should I do?

I returned to Woolworth's and replace my broken gun with the new one.

Now the manager caught me.

Teary-eyed, I explained to him I was actually returning the new gun I had stolen earlier.

I guess the manager believed me. He lectured me on how bad it was to steal and sent me on my way.

Times were much simpler in the 1950s.

• • •

My third grade teacher was Miss Spurr. She was a tough cookie. One morning while reciting the Pledge of Allegiance, I started laughing at a classmate who was making faces. Because I'd been in trouble many times before, Miss Spurr punished me in such a manner that many would consider it to be extreme emotional "child abuse" today.

She made me wear a baby cap and carry a baby bottle around with me all that day in school. I was totally humiliated. During this ordeal, I noticed that one of my classmates, Laura Fleming, was crying on my behalf.

I now know that Miss Spurr thought she was doing the right thing, and I have since forgiven her. But to this very day, Laura Fleming-Carter loathes and has never forgiven Miss Spurr.

• • •

I was heartbroken my fourth grade year when my dog, Butch, was run over by a truck. Though a mutt, he was the smartest dog I ever befriended, or should I say he befriended me. When I rode my bicycle, Butch would jump up, grab the bill of my baseball cap, and run away with it.

He would then set it down a few yards away, waiting for me to retrieve it. When I tried to do so, Butch would pick it up again, dash away and do the same thing.

He was actually teasing me.

Yes, I truly loved my dog Butch.

• • •

Speaking of bicycles, I always liked to ride mine down hills with no hands. I was quite impressed with myself. Though I never got to the bottom of it, I think my dad saw me doing so on several occasions because all of a sudden my bike was gone.

"Somebody must have stolen it," was Dad's explanation.

There was no doubt in my mind that Dad, most likely, gave it away because I was never permitted to acquire another bicycle until my early teens.

• • •

The summer after fourth grade I learned even more about life when I experienced parents getting involved in their children's sports.

I played second base and short-stop on our Little League baseball team, the Comets, that year. Our captain was Wes Tillett, the squad's pitcher. We trained and policed ourselves regarding technique and discipline problems on the squad. All decisions were made on a team-wide basis. At no time was there ever any parent intervention.

Our game uniform included a white t-shirt, with a number on the back and the team's name sewn on the front by our moms. The rest of the outfit consisted of dungarees and sneakers.

Although we weren't the most professionally dressed ballplayers, over half our team later played ball for the high school varsity squad.

Our games were supervised by a teacher, who kept the "stats" which were reported to the local newspaper's sports editor. Our umpire was a high school baseball player who stood behind the pitcher's mound.

My dad (when he could leave his cigar store) was one of the few spectators watching the game from the outfield fence. He never said a word. Moreover, there were very few (if any) arguments during competition.

We were so good that year that we reached the city championship series (best out of three games). We were pitted against a team we never played or had seen before.

Boy, were we in for the shock of our young lives!

Arriving at the field early to warm-up, we were surprised to see a team that was completely attired in baseball uniforms. But what was even more disquieting to us, we saw many adults behind the opposing team's bench and our opponents were being coached by their parents.

We won the first game, but then lost the next two outings and the city championship. That was minor compared to what we witnessed during the course of the event.

From the very first inning of the initial game, all we heard were these father/coaches screaming at their kids and the young umpire.

This display did not only unnerve us, but we genuinely felt sorry for our peers on the opposite side of the field.

Although we were naturally disappointed losing the city championship, we experienced empathy for our adversaries. Our youthful minds conjured up images of our opponents being beaten at home if they would have lost the series.

Since that youthful experience, I have always been wary when parents are coaching their own kids. And over my lifetime I have witnessed, time and time again, parents lose their ethical perspective in their frenzy to make sure their kids won.

•   •   •

Fifth grade was a great year for me; I was on the school safety patrol, and to my recollection I was never paddled that year. Unfortunately, things were quite different for Floyd, who was a sophomore. It started with him playing with matches and accidentally setting our Easter baskets on fire.

Boy, was Dad pissed!

But his troubles got worse during that summer.

Floyd and two friends, Buddy Ehler and Ricky Bernstein, started their own chemistry company. They named it "Welker, Ehler & Bernstein Enterprises, Inc." By using this professional business title, they were able to purchase chemicals that should only be sold to adults.

Their plan was to develop fuel for the small rockets they were designing. Floyd and his fellow scientists performed most of their experiments in the basement of our apartment complex.

Their experimentations stopped abruptly when an explosion in the cellar rocked the entire edifice. Fortunately, no one was hurt and the structure was still intact.

But Dad quickly gathered up all the unused chemical vials and mixtures and sent them back to the chemical company. He also informed them that Welker, Ehler & Bernstein, Inc. was comprised of three underage teenagers. Floyd's days of chemical experiments came to a conclusion.

By the way, I did have the privilege to witness one of Floyd's rockets that actually flew prior to the infamous explosion that ended his career as Werner Von Braun.

. . .

In sixth grade, I learned a lesson I carried with me the rest of my life. On my 12th birthday, Dad bought me a .22 caliber rifle. He wanted to teach me gun safety and how to properly care for a gun.

I would often march up our local coal bank to flat areas where I could set up cans and practice my marksmanship.

On one such shooting session, I happened to spy a young sparrow on the limb of a dead tree about 30 yards away. Thoughtlessly, I wondered, "Could I hit the bird from that distance?"

Impulsively, I aimed and fired. The sparrow died instantly.

At first, I was elated by my sharpshooter skills, but that quickly subsided when I realized I killed an innocent living entity. I then felt extreme remorse and actually prayed to God for forgiveness.

I walked home that day deeply depressed by the senseless killing of the sparrow. I immediately told Dad about my inexcusable murder of one of nature's defenseless creatures.

I gave Dad the gun, vowing I would never touch or fire a weapon ever again. That was a promise I kept the rest of my life. Dad hugged me, knowing how upset I was regarding this transgression.

It was then that I realized how precious life is to all beasts (docile or not) on this beautiful planet we call "Earth."

To this day, I feel regret for my cruel action that ended the life of an animal created by God.

. . .

As I continued to test and learn my limits, my love of nature grew alongside my love of adventure. During my elementary years, Grandfather Bertolette would often take Floyd and me fishing and hiking at a nearby forest that had a small creek running through it. It was great for fishing.

Often Floyd and I would go hiking up the small tree-clad mountain in the area as Grandpa fished. On one occasion when we reached the apex of a hill, we heard the growl of a bear. Floyd and I saw glimpses of it as we tumbled head over heels to the valley below. Floyd lost his bowie knife during our get-away. He's lucky he wasn't impaled by it while rolling down the mountain. We had no intention of going back to look for the knife.

But that was nothing compared to an abandoned, deteriorating red-stone house with black shutters we came across on another hiking exploit. It was located in a clearing where a dirt road led to a back woods county highway.

Surprisingly, the front door was unlocked. The first floor was completely empty, so we decided to venture upstairs. It, too, was empty. But when we opened a closet door, we found a small chest that was locked.

Thinking we discovered a treasure chest, Floyd and I carried it down the stairs and out the front door. We found a long metal bar on the grounds in which we were able to pry open the chest. There was nothing in it but old books, magazines, and newspapers.

Disappointed, we headed back to Grandpa.

On a Sunday two weeks later, Dad was taking the family out to eat at a local Italian family restaurant after church. He took the scenic route through the countryside. Ironically, we passed right by the house we invaded.

There was a police cruiser parked in from of the domicile. Floyd and I looked at each other, swallowed hard, and couldn't wait to reach our destination.

We never talked about that experience again.

• • •

Early in my life, I was diagnosed with OCD…Obsessive-Compulsive Disorder, a neurosis I have had to live with my entire life. It is an emotional anomaly that causes one to dwell on things, be it positive or negative. The disorder is both a blessing and curse for me. A blessing – when working on a project, I never stop until it is completed. A curse – when I have down time, I dwell on negative and self-destructive thoughts.

I was definitely obsessed with the sport of wrestling in which I began training for in elementary school. Nothing else mattered to me, including class work.

Before I continue to share my less than spectacular academic experiences as an adolescent, allow me to digress a bit to illustrate how very important wrestling was to me – and the Welker family.

• • •

CHAPTER TWO

Wrestling: A Welker Family Legacy

"The reward of a thing well done is to have done it."
                                            - Ralph Waldo Emerson

I was always a conservative wrestler. Most of my matches were 5 to 1. Many spectators called me a "staller." I preferred to call it "passive aggressiveness" or protecting a lead.

After I defeated a wrestler from Williamsport, Pennsylvania in the semi-finals of districts my senior year by a single point, his mother and sister actually came into the boys' shower room and screamed at me over the victory. The boy's coach apologized to me following the confrontation. I told him all was fine and I understood their frustration.

Regionals were held at Wilkes College in Wilkes-Barre the next week. I wrestled Bob Ferraro from Easton in the semi-finals, defeating him 2-1. Bob later became a college All-American.

As I was warming up before the finals that evening, a fan said to me, "Welker, do you have your running shoes on again tonight?"

I suppose it motivated me because I crushed my opponent by a score of 14 to 1. Still, those in attendance "booed" me.

It truly is lonely at the top, and it all began for me in 1956.

•   •   •

When I started wrestling in third grade, we had six weeks of training each year. My youth coaches were Elmer Artman, Lou Delbaugh, Joe Cawthern, and Rich Dapra. They were men who loved the sport, not parent-coaches who were there to protect or promote their own kids.

After those weeks of learning mat sense, the high school Key Club had a small tournament for us boys. I still remember getting pinned my very first match by Ray Frederick and Coach Dapra building up my confidence after that defeat. Ray still has that gold medal.

This intramural elementary competition was officiated by high school wrestlers; I was one of those referees years later. The winners and runner-ups each received little gold and silver medals.

It was a low-key, positive experience.

In junior high, we had an outstanding Coach, Charlie Cawthern, who further honed our skills on the mat. Wrestling technique, not winning, was the goal at this level.

However, there was a lot of pressure on me in terms of being a successful high school wrestler. I grew up in the shadow of greatness.

My cousin Harold Welker was a Pennsylvania State Champion in 1938, the first year of the state tournament which was held at Penn State's "Rec Hall." Next, my older brother Floyd did the same there in 1959. I was expected to follow in their footsteps.

But first, I had a confidence problem I had to overcome. They say if you think you are going to lose, you will. Well, I must admit that there were a number of important matches in my competitive wrestling career where I thought I was going to lose prior to competing. But as those bouts unfolded, I began to gradually gain confidence that I could win.

Of course, this feeling of inadequacy contradicts what all athletes have heard from their coaches and motivational speakers forever, "If you want to be a champion, you must first believe in yourself and your competitive abilities."

I guess I did believe in myself, but it was only after the match was in progress and my confidence began to blossom.

Luckily, I removed the monkey from my back when I was crowned state champ in 1963, defeating Sherm Hostler of Newport, Pennsylvania by a score of 4 to 2. A year later, he was a state champion.

I distinctly remember hugging Floyd with tears in my eyes immediately following the victory.

The Welker family name has always been associated with wrestling since the initial Pennsylvania state championships.

•   •   •

I never met my cousin Harold because he died at a very young age. However, I did my homework, talking to his high school friends. I wrote an article about him winning states. The published piece was written as a narrative.

It was a blistery winter Saturday that March of 1938. Harold Welker, a senior for Shamokin High School, was warming-up for his finals match against Angelo Carmella of Dubois. As he looked around the facility, Harold realized that he had never before been in such a huge gymnasium.

It was Penn State's "Rec Hall" and Harold Welker was competing in the first high school state wrestling tournament ever held in Pennsylvania. He was nervous, but not scared. He knew nothing of his opponent except where he was from.

Coach Ken Horner walked over to Harold and said, "It's your turn to win the second individual state championship for Shamokin today. Roland Scandle won at 115, and you can do it at 145. This is important, Harold. You guys will be the first state champions in wrestling. I can sense that this is the beginning of something big.

"Are you ready to make history, Harold?"

"Yes sir."

"Then let's go. You're up."

The match was not an easy one for Harold. Neither wrestler scored a point in the regular match, so the bout would now go into overtime.

During the minute's rest, Harold, breathing heavily, said to Coach Horner, "Give him the freakin' match; I'm too damn tired!"

"That's not going to happen, Harold. Don't quit on me now. This is too damn important. Now get your butt out there and win the match!"

Harold did both.

Thus began the Welker family legacy in the Keystone State.

Wrestling USA Magazine
April 15, 2010 Issue

. . .

As for my brother, Floyd, I only watched him wrestle two matches his entire scholastic career. The reason played out as follows.

Floyd's first varsity home match as a freshman involved a dual meet against Williamsport High School. He was wrestling at the 112-pound weight class.

Dual meets in Shamokin High School's newly-built gymnasium, The Annex, were something special. As I waited for the Shamokin "Greyhounds" to enter the gym for warm-ups, it always amazed me how quickly the gym filled to capacity.

When our team finally came crashing through the paper-woven banner, meticulously manufactured by the cheerleaders, they had to run through a gauntlet of fans to reach the mat. The din was ear-shattering.

The precision in which our team warmed up always intrigued me, and I couldn't wait to be part of the action someday. I took pride in watching my older brother warm-up with the varsity squad.

When the match started, Floyd did not have much time to loosen up behind the team bench because our 95-pounder and 103-pounder both gained quick pins, and the home contingency went wild.

Floyd looked a little nervous to me. But that was to be expected, being his first varsity match.

His opponent was Dennis Slattery, a veteran varsity performer for Williamsport High School, who was no slouch on the mats. But my older brother would show him what wrestling against Shamokin was all about.

As a little kid, the cheerleaders befriended me and I got to sit with them by matside. When Floyd walked onto the mat, the cheerleaders began to chant, "Welker, Welker, he's our man. If he can't do it, nobody can…" I was chanting along with them.

At the shrill sound of the referee's whistle, Floyd attacked like a viper and scored the first takedown. Slattery, likewise, quickly escaped, a bit stunned by Floyd's aggressiveness as a newcomer. The rest of the period was filled with takedown shots and counters.

Slattery had the choice in the second period, and chose the top referee's position.

On the whistle, Floyd hit a sit-out, but sat-out too far. This was Slattery's opening. He snapped Floyd back, forcing his shoulders to the mat. Before

Floyd could react, Slattery cradled him and within seconds the referee slapped the mat, signaling a pin.

The stands on our side suddenly grew silent, as the Williamsport fans were uproarious over the fall.

I never saw Floyd walk off the mat because I went running from the gym in complete despair. My big brother got pinned!

As I ran along the railroad tracks to my home a half mile away, tears were flooding my eyes. You must understand I worshiped my brother and couldn't stand the thought of watching him lose.

Many irrational thoughts ran through my mind. Maybe it was my fault; maybe I was bad luck, a jinx, for Floyd.

Anyway, from that point on, I swore I would never watch Floyd wrestle again. Instead, I waited at home to find out how my brother did.

Actually, I did watch him one more time.

It wasn't until Floyd's junior year that I again built up the courage to observe him wrestling once more. Here's how it all came to be.

For two years my brother had lost three times to an outstanding wrestler, Bill Hughes, from Muncy, Pennsylvania – and the score in the closest match had been 5-1. Hughes, a senior that year, was picked (by coaches and sportswriters alike) to be the state champion in the same weight class as Floyd. So he would have to face the invincible Hughes during the finals of the district tournament and only the winner would advance to the next level of competition.

In the district semi-finals, Floyd won a very tight match, but at the expense of a sprained neck. Between sessions, Dad applied hot towels to the back of his neck to relieve the pain and tenseness.

During the procedure, Dad suggested that maybe Floyd shouldn't wrestle in the night's finals against Hughes, a very physical wrestler who took no pity on anyone who dared to challenge him. Floyd would hear none of that. Furthermore, he told me to come to the match because he wasn't going to lose to his nemesis again.

Although I was hesitant at first, I ultimately went to the district championship finals.

The Annex gymnasium that night was filled beyond capacity, with standing room only. A solitary spotlight illuminated the entire glossy surface of the squared mat located in the center of the arena.

Groping my way in the darkness under the bleachers, I reached a corner of the gym where the parallel bars were situated. With the help of some friends, I balanced myself on the top of one bar, leaning against the wall, so I could see the mat above the many heads of those standing.

While my brother was warming up for the 120-pound match, I glanced at Hughes in the shadows, remembering how strong he was, and realizing Floyd had never managed to score anything but an escape against him. I then heard someone yell, "Hey, Hughes, kick Welker's ass again."

Yet, Floyd told me to come to the gym and assured me that I wouldn't be disappointed.

"And now, ladies and gentlemen, wrestling in the 120-pound championship match from Muncy . . ." The match was about to start and at that point I considered the possibility of vacating the facility, but it was too crowded and too late.

The whistle had blown to begin the first period and Hughes shot in on Floyd with explosive force. Hughes nearly scored a takedown, as they plummeted out-of-bounds.

After that, the majority of the period was loaded with surprising attacks and stunning counters from both mat men. And the spectators were screaming for points!

As the climax of the period approached, Hughes feigned a double leg and slid in for a slick single leg, securing a takedown. Instantly, Floyd recovered with an escape. At the end of the first period, it was 2-1 in favor of Hughes.

Starting the second period, Hughes chose the top position, and within two seconds Floyd procured another escape. The next minute found both grapplers embraced in a mortal struggle for dominance. The onlookers had now transformed into primordial beasts, howling for the kill of one or the other predator battling viciously on the luminous center circle.

I nearly fell from the parallel bar when Floyd almost scored with a dazzling double leg, only to receive the most excruciating cross-face he ever encountered, drawing blood from his nose. In a flash, Hughes reacted with a brilliant arm drag, scoring another takedown. He was truly an amazing machine on his feet.

Moments later, Floyd scored an escape, which was of little consolation to him. The announcer broadcasted a 4-3 lead for Hughes at the close of the second stanza.

Then the unusual happened; Floyd chose the down position at the beginning of the final period, a strategic "no-no" in the 1950s. Floyd's coaches were not pleased with the decision at all. But as before, upon the referee's whistle, Floyd scored with a basic stand-up escape (4-4).

Immediately, the spectators were on their feet, sensing the possibility of a very unexpected upset. But it was short-lived when Hughes executed a picture-perfect, ankle-pick takedown (6-4). Performing a snappy sit-out series, Floyd notched another one-point escape (6-5).

The action that followed was consumed with some of the greatest offensive tactics and defensive maneuvers ever witnessed by these central Pennsylvania wrestling fans.

With less than 20 seconds left in the bout, Hughes drop-stepped back, faked a tie-up, shot in deeply for a double leg, meeting a ravaging inside elbow to the face, as the two mat men careened out-of-bounds. No one scored.

Returning to the 10-foot circle, Hughes felt a warm trickle of crimson oozing from the side of his month; he was really human after all!

It was then that I noticed a look on Floyd's countenance I never saw before, the red-eyed gleam of unbridled determination. At the ref's signal, a sound resembling that of a roar was heard throughout the gym as Floyd penetrated Hughes's defensive perimeter with a tight double leg, lifting him off the mat.

Total silence permeated the gym. Time, for just an instant, stopped. And for that brief moment in athletic history, Floyd was the greatest wrestler in the world.

Floyd rallied from behind to score the final, devastating takedown, winning the match 7-6. All those in attendance gave both gallant gladiators on the glistening mat a five-minute standing ovation, and I surfaced from the pandemonium to hug my idol.

Everyone present believed that they had just observed the state championship match two weeks early, and they weren't wrong. Floyd easily swept through regionals and states, winning the coveted state championship trophy.

Though you may not believe this, I never watched my brother wrestle thereafter. I had no need to because I witnessed him at his very best. For you see, Floyd Robert Welker reached his "moment of mat magnificence" on a chilly March evening in 1959.

• • •

Floyd and I had two hall of fame, high school coaches – Mal Paul and Lyman "Beans" Weaver, who were the perfect combination of a coaching team. They played the old "good cop, bad cop" routine with their wrestlers.

But most importantly, we wrestlers obeyed their every directive. They were tough and unyielding mat mavens.

Coach Paul was a strict taskmaster. His varsity practices were grueling and he put up with no excuses when it came to his rules. He had absolutely no favorites.

• • •

As a youth wrestler, I heard many stories about the "Legend." The one account I will never forget involved Duane McKitrick, an outstanding wrestler. He was undefeated and destined to win states as a junior. Duane was a couple pounds under weight for his weight class the Friday night before districts. But at district weigh-ins he was two pounds over weight. Thus, Duane was ineligible to wrestle in the event.

Coach Paul was furious and denied Duane McKitrick his varsity letter. Duane did not come out for wrestling his senior year.

Though Coach Paul's treatment of Duane McKitrick may seem too harsh in today's society, you must understand that not making weight for any meet was taboo back then – and we all knew it.

I almost shared the same fate as Duane did my sophomore year. Wrestling at 95 and 103, I finished the regular season with a 15-1-1 winning record. I planned to compete at 95 pounds in the sectional tourney. I had one weakness; I liked to eat and came into practice that Monday before the competition well over weight.

Since I only had four days of practice before Friday night's sectionals, Coach Paul bluntly suggested that I move up to 103. I quickly responded, "No, coach, I'll make weight. I can win states at 95. I promise I'll be down by Friday."

"You better be!" responded my irritated coach. I was well aware of the consequences if I didn't make weight.

On Friday night, I qualified for the 95-pound weight class at the sectional championships. As a matter of fact: I was two pounds under weight!

Coach Paul was impressed.

• • •

As a wrestler under his tutelage, I witnessed Coach Paul kick Gene Neyman, a senior varsity wrestler, off the team just for hearing that Gene was smoking. He showed no mercy when one broke the rules. No exceptions.

During dual meet action, Coach Paul wore a three-piece suit. He never argued an official's questionable decisions when they went against us. He was a total professional in the public's eyes.

However, after each of us wrestled, we had to sit by his side where he would quietly critique our performance on the mat. The lewd language Coach Paul used in his review of our mistakes would make a sailor blush.

Practices after dual meets were quite entertaining. His lectures were very flamboyant and filled with sarcastic language. We had to bite our tongues for fear of laughing.

One wrestler, Mike Pufnock, had the physique of an Adonis. Coach Paul was not happy with Mike's actions during one dual meet. After lambasting Pufnock's performance, Coach Paul concluded, "Pufnock, you have arms on you like a blacksmith and use them like a fairy!"

On another occasion, Coach Paul told his nephew, Bob Christ, who wrestled at 145 pounds, "Christ, if you would spent less time sniffin' girls' bicycle seats and more time practicing, you would have a winning record!"

As I'm sure you surmised, Coach Paul was also human with faults and prejudices prominent back in those days. At one practice, Martin "Marty" Winnick and I were working out together. It was near the end of practice and we were half-heartedly going through our moves.

Coach Paul stepped in and began whipping Marty with his leather lanyard, asserting, "You people, I just don't understand you people."

Both Marty and I knew that "you people" was an anti-Semitic statement.

Yes, Marty was Jewish. Still, Martin Winnick has always had the utmost respect for Coach Paul, understanding the intolerances of the time in which we grew up.

There is one humorous match-related incident I want to share. We were wrestling Berwick, Pennsylvania. At the start of the third period, I was about to be placed in the down position.

As required, I looked over to Coach Paul and Coach Weaver for hand-gesture instructions. Coach Paul signaled a "Stand-Up," while Coach Weaver indicated a "Switch."

I was confused as to which maneuver to execute; we never defied our coaches' directions. With only moments to solve my dilemma, I figured out the answer.

At the whistle, I hit a "Standing-Switch," pleasing both coaches.

Coach Paul and Coach Weaver have both passed, but anybody who has ever wrestled for them will never forget the dynamic influence they had on our lives.

They taught us two very important character traits: perseverance and accepting responsibility for our actions.

• • •

I was also very impressed with the honorable referees of our day, especially hall-of-fame official, Glenn Flegal; he was a true master of the mats. Likewise, I never thought of a wrestling official as being the enemy, but rather a friend. Back then, referees were attired in black shoes and pants as well as a long-sleeved, white formal shirt with a black bow-tie.

I was always intrigued with the official's role in policing the mats during dual meet or tournament action. It was then that I decided to don an official's uniform someday.

My coaches even let me referee our team's wrestle-offs for the varsity and junior varsity squads. I suspect they saw a future arbiter of the mat sport in me as well.

• • •

They say that the wrestling room is where champions are developed. That was certainly the case for us. I was pushed by Joe Goguts (my cousin), Rennie Rodarmel, Rich Carter, and Marty Winnick.

Harry Weinhofer, who was a year behind me, was my stiffest competition in practice; we had some great battles during our workouts. Harry was a pinner while I was a takedown artist and rider.

Harry and I only had one wrestle-off; a match in which I won decisively (17-2). I had to make a statement, and I did. Harry never asked for another wrestle-off during our three years together. But he did win states after I graduated.

In dual meets and tournaments, Harry and I were referred to as the "German Dynamic Duo."

My senior year, a gutsy freshman by the name of Joey Bordell had the audacity to challenge Harry and me. We subdued him, but he always came back for more. His senior year Joey became a Pennsylvania state champ.

That's three state champs pounding on each other during each and every practice workout. No one can argue with me that champions are most definitely made in the wrestling room.

•   •   •

As for me, I am most reminded of two wrestling dual meets, where I learned very significant lessons in life. After many victories on the mats, my confidence, which was now full-grown, ironically became an impediment.

The first lesson involved a match in which we didn't listen to Coach Paul's and Coach Weaver's advice. We paid dearly for it, especially me.

To the best of my memory, which is excellent due to my OCD, the competitive experience went something like this.

It was the winter of 1963 in Pennsylvania. The Shamokin High School "Greyhounds" were about to wrestle the Southern Area High School "Tigers" in their yearly central Pennsylvania dual meet. Competing for Shamokin at the time, I (along with my teammates) considered the match to be a "breather" in our otherwise grueling schedule.

Picked to win the contest by an overwhelming margin, our coach and his devoted assistant did everything in their power to temper the overconfidence they sensed in us. We didn't listen and I, in particular, was truly humbled by the experience.

Yours truly was pitted against Tim Steele, a childhood acquaintance who I knew from church. Tim was a nice kid, too nice (I thought) to even consider going out for wrestling. During our coach's pep talk prior to the evening's match, I was instructed to pin Timmy Steele in an expedient manner. Being the defending district champion at that weight class, I fully expected to record the quickest fall of my career.

When Tim and I shook hands at the start of our bout, I was briefly amused by a gleam in his eyes which I mistook as a show of false bravado. At that moment, however, my primary concern was to end the match as swiftly and painlessly as possible.

Ten seconds into the first period, I pancaked Tim, pounding his back to the mat.

It was going to be easier than I previously anticipated. But then, like a flash of lightning, he sprang into a high bridge that almost catapulted me from his body. Tim maintained a steep arch for the remainder of the period, thwarting all my attempts to secure a fall. I was impressed by his tenacity.

Starting the second stanza in the down position, I immediately gained a reversal. Less than twenty ticks later, I placed Tim Steele on his back with a "guillotine."

Like the maneuver suggests, Tim was in agony when I stretched his neck to its legal limit. Still, he fought doggedly to keep his near shoulder off the mat until the period ended.

I was in awe by Tim's incredible defiance of the inevitable. At this point in the match, I was becoming desperate, knowing it was my charge to flatten Tim Steele.

Can you believe it? Even though I was "clobbering" my antagonist, I was the one who began to panic!

On top the third period, I endeavored to crush Tim Steele for putting me through this public embarrassment which I was thus far experiencing. So as soon as the whistle blew, I immediately employed a "Chicken-Wing." (Today, this arm-wrenching hold is outlawed in the mat sport.) With the pressure I applied on Tim's shoulder, I knew he had to be in excruciating pain. Then I shot a devastating half nelson that drove him to his back.

For almost two minutes, Timmy Steele literally cried in anguish. Nonetheless, he never submitted. Then I heard the final buzzer amidst the ear-shattering cheers of those in attendance.

At that very instant, I was visibly stunned by the realization that I had fallen short in accomplishing my goal.

When the referee raised my hand, there was a thunderous round of applause from both sides of the gym. Of course, I understood, as did my coaches and teammates, that the accolades were not for me, but for my valiant opponent.

Although he scored not one point, and was on his back for well over five minutes, Tim Steele was truly the winner of our match.

Southern Area went on to tie Shamokin that night (20-20). It was, without question, a moral victory for the "Tigers." And Timothy Steele was the inspiration behind that surprising outcome.

As members of both squads shook hands at the conclusion of the meet, Tim and I faced each other once again. I smiled with sincere admiration, congratulating him on his fine performance.

There are champions in life very few people remember. I will never forget my competitive encounter with Tim Steele who championed courage.

• • •

Everyone remembers the worst athletic miscues of their entire lives. I am no different. "Stupid is as stupid does" best describes this second lesson I regretfully learned.

It was a frigid January night in 1964 my junior year and we traveled to wrestle Central Columbia, a high school near Bloomsburg, Pennsylvania. The referee was Russ Houk, the legendary wrestling coach at Bloomsburg State College, who was the team manager for the 1960 U.S.A. Olympic Freestyle Wrestling Team.

I was wrestling 112 pounds that year, moving up two weight classes after my state championship performance as a sophomore. My opponent that Wednesday evening was a wrestler by the name of Steve Chamberlain, who was relatively unknown in the mat sport.

I was not at all concerned about my match, and just planned to win and support the rest of my team members the remainder of the dual meet.

At the beginning of the third period, I was winning 9 to nothing, and I was on top. While riding Chamberlain, I got too high. He then wrapped his left arm around my right leg. Thinking he would not know what to do, I leaned my head over his back.

How very foolish.

Before my coaches could scream at me for the mistake, Chamberlain wrapped his right arm around my neck and locked hands, rolling me over to my back. I was entwined in a reverse cradle and there was nothing I could do.

Moments later, Coach Houk slapped the mat, shaking his head in disgust at me.

I was never so humiliated and embarrassed in my entire scholastic wrestling career. My coaches wouldn't even speak to me. I spent the rest of the meet sitting in the chair with my hands on my head.

But it gets even more ludicrous.

Years later, I received a letter from my hometown friend, Ron Weller. In it was a clipping from our local newspaper.

Many news media outlets write columns noted as "What happened this day 10, 20, 30 (and so on) years ago?"

Sure enough, that infamous Wednesday night of long ago was revisited again by my hometown paper in 1994. The headline on the sports page read "Chamberlain Pins Reigning State Champion, Billy Welker in 1964!"

As an English minor, it has forever reminded me of a quote from William Shakespeare's play Julius Caesar, *"The evil that men do lives after them; the good is oft interred with their bones."* So universally and personally true.

•   •   •

As I was learning and relearning humility, I then met an outstanding individual who further ingrained this positive character trait in me.

You will be impressed, too.

Although Floyd and I went to a number of wrestling clinics, my most memorable experience was at Cheshire, Connecticut. It was a ten-day summer wrestling camp.

This wrestling school was located on the grounds of Cheshire Academy, a private school for boys. The man in charge of the dorms during our short stay was Mr. Kelley. He had a great sense of humor. We affectionately called him the "Dean."

Dean Kelley, who was in his late forties, took a liking to us young mat men. So he and his gracious wife invited two other wrestlers and myself to his home for supper.

Dean Kelley was quite the storyteller; he kept us enthralled with his tales of adventure throughout the entire evening.

As we were leaving, I noticed a nifty football statue on his fireplace mantel. I asked, "Dean Kelley, where did you get that super football trophy? It's beautiful!"

He responded, "Oh, I was captain of my college football team and the award was given to me as a senior. No big deal."

Well, I later learned from Dad that the statue was a big deal. The humble man we knew as the "Dean" was Yale's first "Heisman Trophy" winner in 1936 — Mr. Larry Kelley!

•   •   •

Through the wrestling experience, I also learned about the significance of sincere and unconditional friendship.

In life, there have been so-called friends we thought we had, but they disappointed us when we truly needed their help. On the other hand, there are sincere friends we never knew we possessed.

I was blessed with two such individuals. The first was Mark Gerrity, a Shamokin High School underclassman who loved wrestling. He dreamed of becoming a high school teacher and wrestling coach.

I never realized this friendship until Mark and I reconnected in the mid '90s. Since then, I have counted Mark Gerrity as one of my closest confidants, and biggest supporters.

Mark was a sophomore on our wrestling squad when I was a senior. What he remembered the most about upperclassman Billy Welker was that I would spend time talking to him, as well as other younger wrestlers on the team during practices. Something he felt other senior team-members were above doing.

Ironically, I don't remember being nice Mark Gerrity, or anybody else during my junior and senior years on the high school wrestling team.

Personally, I can only recollect being very "moody" from watching my weight, and generally hyper-miserable due to the grueling workouts our esteemed coaches put us through during every practice session.

Upon graduating from Shamokin High School in 1967, Mark Gerrity was drafted into the U. S. Marine Corps and spent two tours of duty in Vietnam.

It cost him his dream.

Returning state-side, Mark had many physical problems due to combat injuries and the infamous Agent Orange. But he still kept a positive, loving attitude on life.

Mark later graduated from Susquehanna University in Selinsgrove, Pennsylvania, receiving magna cum laude honors.

Still, Mark was plagued for nearly 30 years with so many war-related physical complications.

On February 1, 2000, Sgt. Mark J. Gerrity finally succumbed to his wartime ailments. He left a legacy of courage second to none.

Mark's military honors and decorations included a National Defense Service Medal, Combat Action Ribbon, Meritorious Unit Citation, Vietnamese Service Medal with Five Stars, Purple Heart Medal, Vietnamese Cross of Gallantry with a Silver Star, Vietnamese Campaign Medal, Certificate of Commendation, Rifle Sharpshooter Badge, and finally the Navy Commendation Medal with Combat V — the third highest honor given by the Navy!

In the end, Mark Gerrity did accomplish his goal of being a teacher. He taught me the importance of loyalty to one's country and acquaintances throughout life. A valiant warrior, Mark Gerrity was also a gentle man of character. And I have always had more faith in a kind man than I ever had in mankind.

Yes, you never know who your sincere friends really are in life until you need one. To me, Mark was one such friend.

True friendship is a rare commodity – so cherish it!

(Note: On February 26, 2000, Mark J. Gerrity was posthumously inducted into the District IV Pennsylvania Wrestling Hall of Fame for creating the "Pennsylvania District IV Wrestling Website," which was nationally-acclaimed for its innovative and promotional approaches to the mat sport.)

•   •   •

Another high school wrestling peer taught me about perseverance. Our practice room was filled with sectional, district, regional, and all-state wrestlers. At that time, Shamokin, a small high school, had one of the most highly respected scholastic wrestling programs in the Keystone State. Very impressive when one realizes there was only one class of schools in the 1960s (nearly 600 teams), and if you lost at any level of the month-long state elimination process, your season was over. In fact, wrestling was so popular in our area that coal truck drivers actually bet on individual match and dual meet scores.

But of all my outstanding wrestling teammates, I remember Jan Price, a fellow senior, the most. He was one of my closest friends on our high school's wrestling team.

It wasn't until later in my life that I realized what an inspiration Jan was to his fellow teammates regarding individual persistence.

During his four years as a high school wrestler, Jan never missed a practice, never placed in a tournament, rarely won a bout, and never wrestled a single varsity match. But most admirably, Jan Price never quit the wrestling team. Jan's athletic determination has inspired me throughout my entire life.

As a coach, years later, I have had many Jan Prices on my wrestling rosters. I was always impressed with their tenacity. They worked with intensity at practice, pushing the varsity performers to their limit. Their only reward was watching their varsity counterparts succeed in competition.

These wrestlers (the likes of Jan Price) have made such an impression on me that I wrote the following poem dedicated to such inspirational competitors.

THE CHAMPION'S CHAMPION

He's the one loved by his peers,
Though on the bench — he always cheers,
He keeps the first man on his toes,
And never quits — why, no one knows.

•

He puts the champion where he's at,
By making him work to earn his plaque,
His name's not found in big headlines,
But he's always there come practice time.

•

I often wonder — were the champion second team,
Would he keep on trying or lose his gleam,
Would he give his all if there was no fame,
And not give up for the good of the game.

•

There are no questions in this man's mind,
The Champion's Champion — in life — will do just fine.

•

Yes, these special athletes are the ones who later succeed in their chosen professions because they have learned to stay the course without any glory during their school days. They are the unnoticed heroes on all athletic teams who win as adults.

•   •   •

Mom and Dad were proud of our accomplishments on the mats. Floyd and I learned so much from them. Dad taught us about life and Mom taught us about God.

Mom was very big on prayers. When it came to athletic competitions, she taught Floyd and me how to pray.

"Never pray to win; God has no favorites. Instead, pray to do your best and that neither you nor your opponent will be harmed in any way."

She was a saint.

I can't speak for Floyd. Though I definitely know, he too, believes in Mom's prayers since he walked away untouched from a car that he totally demolished.

As for me, I truly believe that Mom's prayers had a lot to do with me not getting into more trouble in my life than I did.

Both Floyd and I were state champions and state runner-ups as seniors. Mom often said to us how pleased she was that one of her sons did not do better than the other as wrestlers – Floyd and I quietly disagreed with Mom.

But how could Floyd or I override the power of her prayers for us. Her devotion to God was nonpareil.

•   •   •

CHAPTER THREE

My Scholastic Years

"Every man is the architect of his own fortune."
- Sallust

I sincerely apologize for the digression. But it is imperative that you realize how significant a role wrestling has always played in my life.

My rocky road as a scholastic student-athlete in grades seven through twelve was filled with many pitfalls.

I must admit I enjoyed my junior and high school years very much, which was monopolized with sports and socializing. But during those days, I didn't know how to study. It was absolutely my fault, not my parents.

•   •   •

I was everything but a model student-citizen during my scholastic days in the school setting.

I was very depressed my first days as a seventh grader. The transition from grade school to junior high was quite a jump for me. I often silently cried at my homeroom desk in the back of the classroom. It was my OCD kicking in. After about a week, I finally became acclimated to my new environment.

•   •   •

I went out for football that fall. I was by no means going to make a name for myself on the gridiron. Here's how that athletic experience went.

I had one physical problem as a football player. I only weighed 75 pounds. But that didn't stop me from trying out for defensive middle (or nose) guard.

Needless to say, I did not fair out too well in that position. Truth be said, I wasn't very good at any spot on the squad. During my two years on the middle school squad, I rarely saw any competitive action. I guess the coach was afraid I would get hurt due to my size. Still, the other members of the team respected me.

Here's why.

At the beginning of every practice, the team would depart from the bus and run two laps around the perimeter of the field (approximately one-half mile). I was always first over the finish line. And the coach often had me lead the warm-up and finish-up exercises because I never missed a single practice session.

On those rare occasions when I did get in the game, I would be dragged by my much larger opponents until one of my teammates assisted in making the tackle. That was the extent of my glory days as a football player, but my coach never forgot my perseverance on the field.

My junior high school football coach often mentioned my name years later when some talented football player was loafing at practice or during competition. Well, I guess I did make somewhat of an impression on him.

If nothing else, playing football in seventh and eighth grade toughened me up for wrestling – my athletic forte.

• • •

The summer between my seventh and eighth grade years my father had me work a couple hours a day in his cigar store at 50 cents an hour. I learned how to "jerk" soda and prepare sundaes (such as CMP's and VMP's). I also memorized the prices of tobacco products and how to properly manipulate that old cash register. It actually helped me in math.

My ultimate goal was to save up enough money to buy a used television for my bedroom.

Although the store was frequented by white collar professionals, many of our patrons were coal miners who looked like Al Jolson. They were covered from head to toe with coal dust. They also had a command of the more vulgar language found, or maybe not found in the dictionary.

There was one awkward situation I experienced in this salesmanship capacity. A customer leaned over and whispered in my ear something I couldn't understand at first. I asked him to repeat himself, but I still couldn't make out what he was saying. Finally, he spoke in a clear voice, "I want to buy a pack of rubbers."

Oh yes, I grew up quite a bit that summer regarding "manly" stuff, and the television looked great in my bedroom.

• • •

When it comes to socializing in high school, my friends and I spent lots of time at local dances. We would travel all over the region to enjoy the activity and, without a doubt, meet as many girls as we possibly could. Our dancing hang-outs included "The Mine" in Mt. Carmel, "Knoebel's Grove" in Elysburg, "Rolling Green" in Selinsgrove, and "Willow Lake" near Pottsville.

We were all pretty good dancers. As for me, my specialty was the "jitterbug," which kept me on the dance floor for hours. Girls in my era appreciated guys who could jitterbug.

I have to thank Susie Jepko for my jitterbug skills. She taught me all the steps needed to perfect the dance.

• • •

I am reminded of two harrowing experiences I had traveling to the various dance locations.

I was driving my dad's Buick to Willow Lake, which was about 45 miles away. There was a new band playing there, The Jordan Brothers. Their live music was the best in the area.

My buddies and I (There were five of us.) decided to take a back road there. I was driving about 50 miles an hour with the radio on full-blast. We were all talking above the music about meeting some cute chicks.

I wasn't paying full attention to the road when we were approaching a sharp curve. There was no way I was going to negotiate the almost 90-degree turn.

I slammed on the brakes. We skidded across the road onto a private driveway and into the owner's garage.

As good luck would have it, there was no car coming in the opposite direction, and the garage door was wide open with no car in it. Terrified, none of us said a word.

I would have apologized to the residents of the home, but nobody was there. Sweating profusely, I pulled out of the garage and driveway. We continued on our way to the dance with my complete concentration on the road ahead.

It was at that moment I realized that we teenagers were not invincible, as adolescents often tend to think.

Playing it safe, I drove back home on the regular route which was devoid of any sharp turns.

Then there was that second infamous close call in which we tempted fate. Marty Winnick's dad bought him a brand new black Volvo for his sixteenth birthday. We were headed to the dance at Rolling Green which was about a 40-minute drive. There were four of us: Marty, Larry Fetterolf, Joe Taby, and myself.

Well, Marty was determined to show-off his driving skills in his new car. We were behind a semi as we reached the apex of a hill.

Marty said, "Watch this!"

He began passing the truck on the down hill. An oncoming car was approaching up the hill. Marty then hit the gas even harder. Everyone in the vehicle, except Marty, thought the end was near. In our minds, we sincerely believed a head-on collision was inevitable.

By the grace of the Divine – my mother's prayers at work – Marty was able to maneuver the Volvo around the truck onto our lane with only a few feet to spare, avoiding what would surely have been a fatal accident.

I never drove with Marty again, that is, unless I was the driver.

• • •

Regarding discipline in high school, I had some minor issues. Early on, I was dismissed from the chorus as a freshman for excessive talking. My sophomore year the band director asked me to hand-in my "drumsticks" for a couple of minute mistakes.

During the half-time shows at our football games, I made some unnoticed errors in foot-judgment. I would often turn left when the rest of the band went right. (I guess I really did listen to the beat of a different drummer.) The band director also got upset when I would join the rest of the band halfway through parades.

Thus, my band days were short-lived.

Still, my musical career was not quite over. Some of my friends and I actually formed a jazz combo. Leonard Reidinger played sax, Wes Tillett was on the trombone, Joe Taby performed on trumpet, and I was the trap-set drummer. We showed off our musical skills at a couple of our high school dances.

I guess we weren't that good because we were not followed by an entourage or surrounded by groupies. Maybe if one of us had some vocal abilities, we would have attracted more admiration from the opposite sex. Still, we had a lot of fun performing together.

My feelings were deeply hurt my junior year when I was kicked out of the Key Club for poor attendance at meetings and projects. I thought they were my friends.

Come on.

. . .

I had some memory problems my senior year. I would sometimes forget to go to school. On one of those moments of lapsed memory, a friend, Bill Niehoff, decided to play "hooky" with me. Bill lived in the country and rode the bus to school. Upon disembarking the vehicle this particular morning, he by-passed school and headed to my house. (Note: Both my parents were working.)

At noon, we decided to get a bite to eat at a local restaurant, and then take a commuter bus to Mount Carmel (seven miles away) to hook-up with a couple girls we knew. As we passed the local post office, we were dismayed when Principal Readly walked out of the building, looking straight at us.

I quickly informed the school administrator that I was sick in the morning, and that I was planning to head back to school that afternoon.

The principal rolled his eyes.

Bill had a more serious dilemma since he lived in the country. He honestly said to the principal, and I quote: "I wasn't sick this morning, Mr. Readly, but I am now."

We both were suspended from school for three days, but it hurt when the principal told my friend, and I quote: "Stay away from Welker!"

I didn't mean to get into trouble or wanted to have a bad reputation. But it felt like I often fell into the spider's web of school-time misdeeds. It was no wonder the principal didn't think kindly of me.

. . .

For the most part, I was pretty well behaved after school, except for a couple of minor incidences on and off school grounds with the local law enforcement officials.

I ran every night during wrestling season and would end my jogging by the Annex gym. While there, I knew how to open the locked side doors to the gymnasium.

Why did I do this? To steal something? No way!

I went there to climb the rope in the gym with only a dim street light as my guide in the darkness. I climbed the rope two times in a row, without using my legs. It was quite a foolish act when you think about it. If I would have fallen, nobody would have known about it until the next morning.

It was a nightly ritual during wrestling season. I had to do it, remember my OCD. Those of us who have OCD tendencies have daily routines we must fulfill. If not, we become very anxious.

Well, one night I couldn't open the door. I became so frustrated that in a fit of anger, I smashed the glass of the door with my foot to get into the gym to complete my physical commitment.

Sad to say, on my way out, the local police were waiting for me. I guess there was an alarm of some sort or someone witnessed my break-in.

They took me home and explained my indiscretion. My dad was irate. You see, he was on the local school board and also its president at the time. I had to use money I saved to make retribution for the property I vandalized.

I surmised that they learned why I was breaking and entering the gymnasium because I didn't receive any further punishment. I suspect it was also due to my father's influence on the school board.

They say it pays to know the right person.

•   •   •

Dad bought me a car known as a Metropolitan my senior year. It was a cute little two-seater. I forget what make it was.

Throughout many school days, I would borrow dimes from my fellow classmates. By day's end, I would have collected about five dollars. It was enough to fill up my car. Oh yes, back then gasoline was only twenty-five cents per gallon.

To this day, I owe many of my fellow high school classmates hundreds of dimes.

After school, I would spend the time buzzing around town with a buddy or two if we could squeeze him in.

While cruising, we listened to the sounds of the Beatles and the Rolling Stones on the radio. British bands were in vogue then at local dances and roller skating rinks. What a great time we had growing up during the 1960s.

As teenagers, we hung out at "Povish's" hoagie and ice cream parlor ran by Helen and Al Povish, who were wonderful people that catered to us kids. Well, one night I decided to show-off in the car. I drove the vehicle on the sidewalk in front of confectionary store and "peeled rubber," with Marty Winnick riding shotgun.

Everyone on the scene of the reckless act loved it.

Moments later, the police pulled me over. An officer who knew me said, "Billy, what the hell do you think you're doing? You could have hit somebody with that stunt. So now we're going to follow you and your contraption home and have a talk with your parents."

I lost car privileges for a month.

.   .   .

My senior French class was right before first lunch; ours was the second lunch period. Well, we convinced our French teacher, Miss Owens, that the bell for the beginning lunch period was ours. So, she would dismiss us. I can't but feel she just wanted to get rid of us misfits; there were a lot of athletic characters in the class.

.   .   .

Did you ever wonder for the last decades why there are no condiments on the tables of school lunchrooms everywhere? Well, it was because of idiots like me. I would loosen the caps of the sugar, salt and pepper holders and watch the shock in the eyes of fellow students as they poured them. I was no good.

But that was nothing. Let me share with you the coup de gras of my lunchroom antics. I had the uncanny ability to make my classmates laugh while eating. During the days when grilled cheese sandwiches were on the school menu, I would stalk students who were eating the sandwiches with chocolate milk.

When they were in half swallow, I would make them laugh. There is nothing like the beauty of watching cheese and chocolate milk squirting from their noses. It was a masterpiece of mealtime misdemeanors.

• • •

Besides competing in wrestling, my dad taught me how to play golf over the years at our local country club. So I finally decided to join the school's golf team as a senior and made the fifth-man varsity slot. That's the lowest, or should I say the highest scoring golfer on the varsity squad, which means I barely made the first team.

During meets between two schools, the first man of one squad plays the top man on the other team, and so on down the line.

Dual matches were scored in the following manner. The first nine holes and last nine holes were scored by match play, the participant who won the most holes in the front nine scored one point and another point could be earned in the back nine. If there was a tie in either nine holes, both golfers would score half of a point.

A final point was scored by medal play, the lowest score. A golfer had the potential to score a total of three points during the 18-hole match.

Competing against the best team in our district, Lewisburg High School, it came down to my fifth-man match to determine if Shamokin could score an upset victory. I won the front nine while my opponent won the back nine.

When we approached the eighteenth hole, players and coaches from both squads surrounded the green. I was one stroke ahead, but I had a long 50-foot putt. My adversary was in the same predicament, a little farther from the hole.

He putted his ball approximately five feet from the hole, looking at a straight putt from there. I succeeded in putting my ball within four feet of the hole, but on a slant.

Putting first, my opponent dropped the ball into the center of the hole. Now the pressure was on me. If I make the putt, we win by a half point. If not, Lewisburg beats us again as they had so many times in the past.

My golf coach, Paul Sabin, had the utmost confidence in me making the putt. He knew I was very often involved in pressure situations for years on the mats, prevailing under such stressful athletic circumstances the majority of the time.

It was a delicate putt. The hole was on a slight slope and there was a sharp break to the right. If I hit the ball too soft, it would break too soon, missing the hole in front. Should I tap the ball too hard, it wouldn't break enough and roll above and beyond the hole.

To say the least, I was a bit nervous by the athletic situation I faced, and took more time with the putt than I usually did.

I took a deep breath, exhaled and stroked the ball. When it reached the cup, it caught the upper lip, circled around the cup twice before dropping into the hole.

I looked over to Coach Sabin, who had dropped to his knees. Immediately after the putt, I told him no sweat. I think he wanted to choke me for what I put him through those tenuous seconds. Instead, he shook my hand.

I don't know if we ever beat Lewisburg again since that day on the links. But I do know it was my finest hour, ever, on the golf course. To this day, I love golf, but unfortunately, I think it hates me. I'm sure many, who also love the game, sincerely understand my sentiments.

·   ·   ·

As far as knowing what I wanted to do in life, I didn't have a clue. Oh, my grandfather and mother were teachers, but that was the farthest thought from my mind. My father wanted me to consider the law field, but that wasn't in the picture, either.

I know my parents and grandparents were very proud when I graduated at around the top 50-percent of my class that May. Despite my blasé academic record, I could tell that they were happy because I heard their sighs of relief.

·   ·   ·

Due to my wrestling prowess, I received an athletic scholarship from the University of Pittsburgh. When my high school guidance counselor learned I was accepted at Pitt, he called me into his office. To this very day, I remember his words of encouragement: "Welker, you won't last a semester at Pitt!"

I was inspired.

So off to college I went in the fall of 1965.

·   ·   ·

CHAPTER FOUR

My Undergraduate Years: A Time of Turmoil

"I am the master of my fate . . ."
                                        - William Ernest Henley

Building on the strong foundation from my parents, coaches and teachers, I was now stepping out on my own. But I was young, immature, and my mischievous spirit was still strong, so there was going to be a very bumpy path ahead of me.

• • •

My first college semester at Pitt, I considered the field of economics and I passed Econ 101. But that initial economics course just didn't turn me on; in fact, I found it less than intriguing. Thus, I was still at a loss regarding a future career. That's a decision I would have to make after completing my required coursework in the liberal arts.

• • •

At Pitt, my first residence was Tower B, one of three round buildings known by the students as Ajax, Babbo, and Comet. At five each night, we would all gather in the tower's commons area to watch two action shows on TV. In vogue during the 1960s were the original "Batman" and "Star Trek" series. We never missed an episode.

By using high-powered flashlights, some of the students in Tower B were able to beam the Batman icon on the outside walls of Towers A and C. This upset the dorm counselors in Tower B. They questioned all of us, but never caught the culprits.

• • •

Gradually my life on the mats started to deteriorate. To begin with, I learned that a fellow freshman teammate received a more comprehensive scholarship than I did. He never won a significant tournament, whereas I was a state champ and state runner-up.

When I confronted the head coach about it, he quite bluntly told me, "If you don't like it, you can leave."

That wasn't in my nature. As I have mentioned a number of times in this narrative, I am OCD, which to me meant you finish what you start. Wrestling-wise I made my point; I repeatedly manhandled the abovementioned mat man my freshman year, but the spark to compete at the collegiate level was beginning to dwindle.

• • •

Our freshman wrestling coach was the legendary Rex Peery. He retired the previous season as head coach, having produced numerous national champions over his 20-year tenure at Pitt.

A three-time national champion from Oklahoma, Rex developed both his sons (Hugh and Ed) into three-time national titlists as well. This unique feat has never been duplicated. And all three, now deceased, were inducted as "Distinguished Members" into the National Wrestling Hall of Fame in Stillwater, Oklahoma.

Although we learned so much from Coach Peery as college newcomers, freshmen at that time could not wrestle on the varsity team. Furthermore, we had no freshmen wrestling schedule, except for the U.S. Naval Academy Freshman Tournament at the end of the season.

We spent the entire season drilling, drilling, drilling without experiencing a real college match, which lasted nine minutes years ago. In high school, bouts are only six minutes. This put us at a handicap when we finally wrestled in the freshman tournament.

My first match at the competition was against a boy from Penn State. Rex Peery sat in the coaching chair. I was a dynamo the first two rounds of the match, leading 14 to 1 at the end of the second period.

Perceiving an easy victory for me, Coach Peery left my match to assist one of my fellow teammates wrestling (and on the verge of losing) at another mat.

After my match, Rex asked, "Did you pin him?"

"No coach, I lost 15 to 14."

"What!"

"I ran out of gas, coach. It's like I hit a brick wall."

Coach Peery was not happy, and neither was I, but for a far different reason. The boy from Penn State was prepared to wrestle a nine-minute match, having done so throughout the course of the season. I was not; it was the first college bout I ever wrestled.

We should have had a freshmen wrestling schedule that year. I know the outcome of my match would have been quite different with previous exposure in wrestling nine-minute bouts.

Although I placed in the tournament, the experience further dimmed my desire to continue competing in the sport.

•   •   •

Another experience that further dampened my enthusiasm to continue competing in the mat sport landed me in the hospital.

The summer after my freshman year I bought a small motor cycle. The first night I had the two-wheeler, I gave my mother a ride on it. A car pulled out in front of me. I swerved to miss it, but instead of hitting the brake, I punched the accelerator. The bike careened into Wolf's store window where I banged my head into the glass, breaking it.

Mom was in a panic and ran home (a block away) to get Dad. Meanwhile, I was bleeding above the eye and my right leg was cut up badly. I remember an onlooker saying, "Is there a priest to give him last rites?"

I thought I was blind in one eye, but it was just blood covering it. The next thing I was conscious of was Mom and Dad being by my side. From there, it was off to the local hospital.

After a three-hour operation, I spent 10 days in the hospital; it was one of the worse experiences in my life. I was put in a ward with others, some of them dying of a myriad of sicknesses. I wanted so badly to be out of the hospital that I couldn't sleep at night. When I was finally released, I was in the state of extreme emotional discomfort. To this day, I have a phobia for hospitals.

•   •   •

Wrestling in high school prepared me to persevere. My sophomore year at Pitt money was, more often than not, tight for me. To make up for it, I was on the clean-up crew after football games at Pitt Stadium on "Cardiac Hill." I was also a lifeguard at the university's Olympic-sized pool in Trees Hall. On a five-dollar bet, I attempted to perform a one-and-a-half off the 10-meter diving board. By the Unseen Power, I'm lucky I didn't kill myself … walking away with five bucks.

Another source of income was selling my blood at the Pittsburgh Blood Bank every 11 weeks for ten dollars, a donut and orange juice.

During the beginning of wrestling season my sophomore year, I sold blood one Saturday morning prior to us having a scrimmage wrestling match with Clarion State College (now Clarion University).

My bout with one of the Clarion "Golden Eagle" wrestlers ended with me defeating him barely by one point. After the match, my head coach was concerned with my performance.

"Bill, you look very pale. What's the problem?"

"Coach, I sold a pint of my blood for 10 bucks. I needed the money."

"Why didn't you tell me; I would have given you the money."

Learning to be on my own in the big city, I never thought of asking anybody for money, especially my head coach. After all, he told me my freshman year if I didn't like the fact that a lesser wrestler received a better scholarship than me, I could leave.

Though struggling money-wise at Pitt my second year, I had too much pride in asking my parents or anyone for financial help.

I was basically on my own and wanted to make it on my own. The high school days were over. Still, I would continue to make irrational decisions that I would have to live with the rest of my life.

•   •   •

My sophomore year I made the varsity wrestling team at Pitt, defeating a senior on the squad. That season I came to the realization that I was a good wrestler, not a great one.

Although I was solid when it came to technique, I lacked two important traits – a mean-streak and being physical on the mats – important assets needed to be a successful Division I wrestler.

Finally, I completely lost the desire to compete in the mat sport. I was no longer interested, tired of dieting, and was kicked off the team when I started smoking and consuming alcohol in excess.

• • •

Then another blow: My girlfriend at the time sent me the proverbial "Dear John" letter. The communiqué was a deep emotional downer for me. I went steady with her for about three years. She shunned me for a guy who lived in the Harrisburg, Pennsylvania area near where she worked. They married the following summer.

And that was that.

During my personal pang over the break-up, I thought about a wonderful girl two years behind me in high school. She had a crush on me, and I often saw her upset in my presence. As a matter of fact: After being kicked to the curb by my girlfriend, I saw her one more time. She read me the "riot act." I wanted to say that I knew how she felt, but instead, I just stood there and took her very descriptive verbal lashing.

What moxie!

• • •

To make matters worse, my grades were suffering. It was during this time that I had my first bout with depression. At night in my dormitory room, my tears soaked the pillow. I was in a dark place and I desperately needed a turning point – some help. Although my father raised me to be self-sufficient and my mother was perpetually praying on my behalf, I still felt lost. My life was falling apart.

• • •

I was like a zombie when I attended classes. I was failing French, probably due to my shenanigans in our high school French class which came back to haunt me.

As my world began to collapse under me, I then created more problems for myself in Tower B. It was right before Thanksgiving and I was planning to go home for the holiday.

The big event of the weekend was our annual football game between Shamokin High and Mt. Carmel High, an area school that was a perennial powerhouse on the gridiron.

While I was packing that Tuesday afternoon, I placed a pint of whiskey that a senior purchased for me on the top of the clothes I was taking home. Just then, our dorm counselor, Clancy, walked into the room. I forget his last name, but he was actually from Mt. Carmel and was very familiar with our local football rivalry.

"What are you doing with that whiskey? You know alcohol is not allowed in the towers."

"I'm taking it home for our Thanksgiving football game against your high school. Besides, it's not even open, Clancy."

"Give it to me, now!"

"Are you serious?"

"Absolutely."

He confiscated my bottle and left the room, but he never reported me to the Dean of Student Housing that day. I suspected he kept it for himself.

On Wednesday morning, I had an early 8:00 am English literature class. After that, I planned to go back to my room, get my stuff and go home.

As I exited the elevator on my floor, I thought to myself, "Did Clancy take my booze to the dean? I don't think so."

I saw a maid, and told her I locked myself out of my room. She opened the door, but it was not my room; it was Clancy's. I thanked her as she left.

Surveying the room, at first I found nothing. Then I looked in the cabinet next to his desk. There it was, my pint of whiskey still not opened. I took it and left the room, locking the door.

I went back to my room, put the whiskey bottle in my suitcase and headed home for the weekend.

Upon returning to Pitt the next Monday, I went to all my morning classes.

But when I returned to my room at noon, I was immediately informed by Clancy to report to the housing dean's office on the first floor. He smiled as I left him.

When I reached the Dean of Student Housing's office, the name on the door was Mr. Goldberg. As I entered, the dean told me to sit down in front of his desk. It felt like my life couldn't get worse.

"Mr. Welker, did you enter Clancy's room under false pretenses and take your pint of whiskey?"

"Yes, I did, sir."

"Did you have any idea what the consequences would be?"

"No sir."

"Well, it's serious. You're going to be expelled from the dorms. But not only that, higher ups wanted to kick you out of Pitt."

In a state of disbelief, I said, "I can't believe it! What am I going to tell my parents? My dad will kill me!"

"Well, I talked my superiors into just removing you from the dorms."

"Thank you. My parents would have been very unhappy."

"Billy, it is Billy?"

"Yes sir."

"Now it's up to you to get your act together. How are you doing in school?"

"Not so good, and I'm failing French."

"Can you find anywhere else to live?"

"Yes, at my fraternity house."

"When you get yourself settled in your frat house, I want you to come see me."

"I will."

When I returned to Dean Goldberg's office, I was completely surprised. He actually began tutoring me in French. Because of his help, I passed French that semester.

At the time, I couldn't understand why this man was so worried about me; he didn't know anything about me. But still he cared about my future. Though I never saw him after that school term, I will always remember his kindness. Maybe Dean Goldberg also surmised Clancy's true intentions regarding that bottle of whiskey.

• • •

My parents never found out about my dismissal from the school dormitory. It was entirely my problem; my father ingrained in me to accept responsibility for my actions – good or bad.

After I was able to find refuge in my fraternity house, I informed Mom and Dad of my new domicile. They never questioned why I moved there.

• • •

During the spring semester of my sophomore year, I selected education as my major, specifically physical education. After all, my life always revolved around sports – wrestling, baseball, football, golf, shooting pool, tennis, bowling, etc.

My grades began to improve since I refocused my OCD priorities on academics rather than athletics. Though very difficult at first, I gradually learned how to study and take appropriate recitation and lecture notes.

• • •

My burgeoning study skills met challenges. During a review of a United States history final exam I was about to take, our recitation professor told us what specific topics we should study for the test. There was a problem, though. Another professor in the Pitt history department developed the evaluation.

Upon perusing the test, I realized that none of the essay questions were ever emphasized in my class. I must confess, for a moment, I was in a state of panic.

But then I was reminded of a quote from my Grandmother Bertolette – a firm believer in God and the power of positive thinking. She shared with me her thoughts on life: "Billy, no matter how bad a situation seems, the sun will come up in the morning."

Consequently, I opened the final exam blue book and wrote a brief note to my recitation professor, explaining my dilemma. Then, I developed essay questions of my own, answering them with everything I studied for the test. It paid off.

Even though I did not answer a single essay question on the test, my reward for this effort of last resort was an "A" in the course. I suspect my recitation professor was impressed with my ingenuity.

• • •

But I was still on a downhill spiral regarding my personal lifestyle. I was lonely and committed many acts of stupidity that I am ashamed of to this very day.

Talking about being incredibly asinine, I was taking an evening educational history and philosophy class which was attended by about 300 undergraduates. I sat in the very back of the lecture hall, drinking cans of beer I had in my briefcase while taking notes. Ironically, on the midterm and final exams, I scored one of the 10 highest grades in the course, receiving an "A+."

A couple of guys that witnessed my unique note-taking strategy in the class and received "B's," jokingly asked what brand of beer I drank. I guess they thought it might improve their grades.

· · ·

The summer was a welcome break from school – a time to refocus my energies and make money. I gained employment with the Jones and Laughlin Steel Mills in the Pittsburgh area.

That summer I lived in Ambridge at the home of a retired matron across the Ohio River from Aliquippa where the steel mill was located. I had to take a municipal bus to the job each day.

I worked as a lid man on top of the coke ovens for a while. That stopped suddenly when the wind changed and the flames on top of the oven slightly scorched my face. The foreman immediately reassigned me to another job, cooling the red-hot coke with water hoses. I guess he didn't want a college kid dying on his watch. I was grateful for the change.

One day at work my foreman asked if I'd pull a double (16-hour) shift. It was fine with me since I had nowhere to go, except to my room in Ambridge. After the double, as usual, I rode the bus home, falling asleep. When I woke up, I was back at the mill again. That's how extremely tired I was.

The days that I had off, I would frequent a neighborhood bar, where they had no problem serving beer to a minor.

I must also acknowledge that I tried marijuana twice that summer, and I inhaled. However, the two reefers did nothing for me. So, I passed on the "free love" generation's drug of choice, though I had no qualms with free love. Likewise, with the way my luck was going, I probably would have been arrested for possession if I would have been turned on to weed. I finally made a righteous decision.

Overall, it was a lonely summer in Ambridge with no friends to hang out with. The only upside, the pay was great. I was able to save up enough money to pay my tuition for the year, as well as daily expenses. Mom and Dad always paid the rent wherever I was staying during my college days.

· · ·

When I received a long weekend from the mill, I went home to visit Mom and Dad. I also hung out with a few of my buddies.

Some of the insane things we did, one would not believe.

A college acquaintance of mine loved to drive large vehicles. He was a member of a local community's volunteer fire company. We would often drive a hook and ladder fire truck around the area in the middle of night. I was the wheel man at the top.

What a ride!

But it gets even more incredible.

He also enjoyed driving buses. On Saturday nights, a group of us would drive up to where regional public transits were parked. Our leader knew how to enter the bus court and start the buses.

Well, about 20 of us (guys and gals) would embark the bus, carrying a keg of beer on board. We drank for hours as our chauffer drove us all around the countryside.

He returned the bus near dawn, and even knew how to fill it up with petroleum in the bus yard.

I still can't figure out how we got away with it. Again, I guess things were much simpler back then.

• • •

Today, Jones and Laughlin is no longer in existence: the fault of mismanagement and outrageous union demands. The laborers were granted triple time on their birthdays and after so many years of employment they received 13 weeks of paid vacation.

Greed and foolishness on both sides ended it all.

So sad.

Now the only place where you'll find Pittsburgh's "men of steel" is on the football field.

• • •

My life was still in a state of confusion. I had no idea what I planned to do with my life. As they say, "I was trying to find myself," and I felt worthless, continuing to combat depression with alcohol. Of course, it was a futile and negative course of action.

. . .

My struggle seemed to mirror what was happening on campus and around the world. I attended the University of Pittsburgh during the height of the Vietnam Conflict. Pitt being a major university, there were many student protests and demonstrations against the war.

To be quite honest, I didn't know whether the conflict was right or wrong. But what I did know, I had friends over there, including my youth wrestling and high school buddy Ray Frederick – and I totally supported all of them.

There were no protests or demonstrations during my daily routine. Besides, my parents didn't send me to college to get involved with political matters. My job was to get an education and graduate as far as they were concerned.

. . .

My confused spiral continued. In the summer, between my sophomore and junior years in college, I was arrested for speeding and lost my driver's license for three months during a long weekend visit home.

Upon returning to Pitt the next fall, I buzzed around the campus in my small motor cycle to attend classes and various school activities.

My next mistake of irresponsibility, I forgot to get the mini-bike inspected. I was pulled over by a City of Pittsburgh police officer for the infraction. Of course, I had no driver's license to show him. He arrested me on the spot.

Next, I was immediately taken in handcuffs to Pittsburgh's Oakland Precinct by the officer.

It was a Friday afternoon. I waited until nearly 9:00 p.m. before I was driven to the Grant Street main police station for arraignment.

As I was led to my holding cell prior to facing the night court magistrate, I was astonished by the grim and atrocious crimes of other detainees, including one individual whose moniker was "Chicken-Man." Don't ask.

Finally, at 2:00 o'clock in the morning, I was brought before the night court litigator. I was given my rights and learned how serious my traffic offense was considered. At that point, one of my college fraternity buddies paid my bail.

Dad had to drive to Pittsburgh to appear with me before the judge a few months later. Surprisingly, my dad was not as upset as I thought he'd be. The verdict was a fine and my license was suspended for one year.

• • •

I had one more encounter with the City of Pittsburgh police, but this time I was the victim, not the culprit.

On rare occasions, I would venture to the Hurricane Club in the Hill District to listen to some great live jazz music by local talented black musicians. It was truly a unique entertainment experience to witness.

Since I lost my license, a fraternity brother drove me there at 9 p.m. and was supposed to pick me up one Saturday evening at midnight. He never showed up and I was alone on the streets of the Hill District, which was not the safest area of the city.

How was I going to return to Oakland and my frat house?

As bad luck would have it, I was approached by a black individual and his female companion. He asked me for my money; I didn't perceive it to be a request. I gave him ten dollars; all I had on me. They then walked away.

Now I was broke and disoriented as to which direction to go. Then a police car pulled up to the curb where I was standing.

The policeman on the passenger's side said, "What the hell are you doing up here at this hour of the night?"

I explained to him everything, including my ten-dollar forfeiture to the black couple.

He told me to get into the cruiser and asked, "Would you know the pair if you saw them again?"

I responded, "Yes."

We drove around for a couple of minutes, and sure enough, we found them. Another cruiser picked the couple up and took them to the Hill District precinct.

They were taken to a back room.

A few minutes later, the officer I spoke to came out of the room and gave me back my ten bucks. He said they weren't going to charge them with anything since it wasn't worth the effort.

"That's fine with me," I said. Then I asked how I could get back home.

He actually drove me in a cruiser back to my fraternity house.

As I got out of the car, the officer quite poignantly stated, "Don't ever come up to the Hill District again! Do you understand me, son?"

I replied, "You can count on it, officer," and then profusely thanked him.

As an afterthought, the reason my frat brother didn't pick me up was quite simple. He didn't forget me; he got drunk and passed out.

Who was I to cast aspersions his way; I forgave him.

. . .

During the summer prior to my senior year in college, my buddies and I devised a plan to crash wedding receptions. We learned where they were going to take place in the Pittsburgh area. If the reception began at 2:00 o'clock in the afternoon, we waited a couple hours before entering the reception hall when everybody there was feeling good. Then we just mingled with the invited guests, drinking, eating and enjoying ourselves. We had it down to an art, often congratulating the bride and groom on their very special day. The ingenious scheme was a blast.

. . .

Life was a mixed bag for me. My grades continued to improve, but I still felt empty, lost and continued to struggle with depression. The bottom line: I had no real social life to call my own, and I was still very lonely.

While it was a challenging time, it was helping me grow as a person. It was the hardest time of my life so far, preparing me for the demands of adult living.

. . .

But my troubles were far from over. In the fall of my senior year, I contracted Mononucleosis. I would sweat copiously at night, seem better in the morning, attend classes, but by the afternoon, I would begin to feel weak, nauseous and feverish. The physical agony lasted for nearly a month.

At the time, I lamented: "How many more problems in my life can I endure?"

. . .

CHAPTER FIVE

Love and Teaching: Finding My Place

*"The two most important days in your life are the day
you were born and the day you find out why."*
                                                    - Mark Twain

Finally, my fortunes were about to change. It was during the Christmas break of my senior year and I decided to go to a dance at the Stan-Lee, a bar in my hometown. I happened to notice a girl I knew from high school, Margaret "Peggy" Bainbridge. And to be more specific, she was the first girl I ever dated. So, I tapped her on the shoulder and asked her if she would like to dance.

She politely answered, "No, thank you."

Another rejection.

So, I decided to buy a six-pack, leave the dance, and again drowned my sorrows in beer and self-pity.

As I was departing, I was tapped on the shoulder. I turned around and the same girl said to me, "Billy, I didn't know it was you. I would love to dance with you."

I was visibly surprised. Little did I know, my path was changing for the better – not for that night, but for the future. I was dancing with the love of my life.

• • •

In the coming days and weeks, Peggy and I caught up. I already knew that her parents had passed away when she was in high school. She lived with her sister until she graduated. After that, she was essentially on her own and had to grow up quickly. She told me she'd been working in the DC area before we reunited. I realized quickly that her personal trials provided Peggy with an inner strength that few possess in life.

Three months after the dance we eloped and were married by a Justice of the Peace in Williamsport, Pennsylvania. That night I took her to the district wrestling championships at Williamsport High School, a facility I had wrestled in many times as a scholastic mat man.

What a honeymoon!

•   •   •

A month after Peggy and I eloped, we went to visit my parents on a sunny Friday. It was then that I informed them that we were married. I knew I would receive Mom's blessing, but I wasn't quite sure what Dad's reaction would be.

Dad was pleased, but also concerned. He had Peggy, Mom, and me sit down at the dining room table with him. At that point, he explained what needed to be done.

First, he wanted us to have a religious wedding as well. He also instructed Peggy and me to go to Shuey's Jewelry Store Saturday morning and select an engagement ring for Peggy, which would be my parents' wedding gift to her.

While we were shopping for a ring, Dad made some phone calls. Since Peggy was Roman Catholic and I was Presbyterian, that afternoon we went to St. Edward's Catholic Church to be married by Father LeRoy Jones, who was assisted by our family minister, Rev. James Mosier.

After the ceremony, Mom and Dad took us out for dinner. We finished the day stopping at a local Dairy Queen to enjoy some soft ice cream.

(Although Peggy was Roman Catholic, she later raised our four children as Lutherans, a compromise between our two religions. It was her decision entirely. My only concern was that they would have a church to go to.)

•   •   •

Back at school it almost felt like life was testing the limits of my newfound good fortune. During the last semester of my senior year, the selective service administration had its first "lottery" to determine who would be drafted into the Viet Nam Conflict. There were no longer any college and marriage deferments.

The lottery process was something like playing bingo. Inside a huge tumbler were 366 ping pong balls with a date inscribed on each one, representing the individual's birth date for all males, ages 18 to 25.

The first 120 birthdays pulled from the drum essentially guaranteed that eligible individuals with those birthdays would be drafted. From 121 to 240, you might be drafted. Males, whose birthdays were the final 120-plus ping pong balls picked, would avoid being drafted at all.

I must admit Peggy and I were anxiously watching the selection process on television that night. It took quite awhile.

My birthday was finally removed from the tumbler as the 320th birth date selected. Peggy and I sighed with relief. Although I would not have avoided the draft, I was so thankful with the outcome.

It's another blessing in my life that can only be attributed to Mom's prayers for me. Yet again, her petitions kept me safe.

Ever since then, I have never won a raffle or lottery. Still, I count myself as one of the luckiest guys on the planet.

. . .

Relieved of the threat of being drafted, I still had business to complete at Pitt. I was finishing my student-teaching obligation in the Pittsburgh Public Schools system. The experience was a disaster. My cooperating teacher at the high school did not appreciate my inability to deal with discipline problems in the classroom.

I received a "B" as a student-teacher, which was considered unheard of in those days. Moreover, my cooperating teacher wrote in his evaluation form of my teaching ability: "Bill Welker might be able to teach in a rural one-room school house…but nowhere else."

Not a very flattering start in the educational profession, but I brushed it off figuring my cooperating teacher didn't like me from the start. Likewise, my mind, energies and personal motivations were on other matters at the time, like marriage.

Nonetheless, I graduated and decided to immediately apply for the "Master of Education Program" at Pitt. The physical education department had an accelerated one-year master's curriculum that was very appealing to me.

Amazingly, I was accepted into the yearlong graduate degree program.

• • •

I started my master's studies in the summer of 1969, and Peggy often attended classes with me. She actively participated in class discussions and projects. This is just one example of how my wife supported me throughout our marriage. Peggy has always been my personal cheerleader and critic.

• • •

That summer I had a part-time position with the physical education department, as an instructor for the "Leisure Learn" recreational program which catered to the general public in the evenings.

In August, one Friday night after work, Peggy (now almost five months pregnant), Rich Carter (my hometown friend visiting us from Wheeling, West Virginia), and I went to the "Swizzle Stix" nightclub. The lounge featured "Gary Glenn and the Soul Set," a local all-white band that exclusively performed James Brown ("The Godfather of Soul") melodies. They had a saxophonist who would perform 15-minute solos. He was fantastic.

I have always enjoyed soul music the likes of the Temptations, Four Tops, Stevie Wonder, Commodores, Rare Earth, Aretha Franklin, Martha and the Vandellas, Mitch Ryder and the Detroit Wheels, Percy Sledge, Kool and the Gang, and on and on. I was most definitely a Motown fan.

After a couple beers, Rich and I happened to notice a girl who was turning down male offers to dance with her. And those guys were dressed to kill. She definitely came off as being very stuck up.

So, being young and only somewhat mature, Rich and I decided to put her in her place: One of us was going to go over to her and ask for a dance. I won the flip. The plan was to tell her "where to go" when she turned down my offer to dance.

Besides, what girl who was dressed to the "T" would want to dance with a guy attired in a cut-off sweat shirt, worn inside-out, sneakers and blue jeans?

Peggy was all for our ingenious idea.

I went right over to her table and asserted, "Would you like to dance?"

Her answer to the request was: "Sure."

Confused by the response, I started to slow dance with her. After all, she was quite a good looker.

Moments later, Peggy, obviously with child, tapped her on the shoulder and asked, "Do you mind if I dance with my husband?"

The girl was so embarrassed that she and her friends quickly left the establishment.

Back at our table, I was profusely apologizing to Peggy. She was far from pleased at first.

Rich laughingly asked, "Billy, why did you dance with her?"

"Rich, I wasn't expecting her obliging answer. And I guess I was flattered. I mean, she turned down all those other guys. My ego took over; I have no other excuse. What would you have done, Rich?"

He didn't respond.

The rest of the night went without any more hitches and Peggy finally forgave me, wisely understanding the psyche of virile, foolish young man.

•   •   •

At the start of the fall term, I was running out of student loan money I received that summer. Being married and with our first child (Billy) on the way, I had to find a full-time day job, pronto.

Thank goodness all my graduate classes were in the evening hours during the fall and spring terms.

Fortunately, I was offered a permanent-substitute position as a physical education teacher at Philip Murray Elementary School in the Pittsburgh Public Schools System. My first professional teaching assignment was unquestionably a baptism of fire.

Through the grapevine, I learned that the teacher, whose position I was taking, was on medical leave due to a nervous breakdown.

Nice.

What was I getting myself into?

The school was located in a very rough neighborhood. The first two weeks teaching gym class I tried to implement teaching strategies I learned in college – be student-oriented, understanding, compassionate, and loving. To use a slang expression: "Ain't none of it worked!"

I knew I had to change tactics or my first position as a professional educator would be a teaching nightmare. Then I remembered what worked on me as a grade school student.

On Monday of the third week, I went to the school office to discuss my dilemma with Principal Kisick. Here's pretty much how the conversation went decades ago.

"Mr. Kisick, I am having discipline problems in my gym classes."

He bluntly stated, "I know, and I'm thinking about firing you."

I responded, "I understand. But before doing so, would you allow me to bring the five or six most difficult students I have in my classes to your office and paddle them myself. If you paddle them, it will not help my problem. It has to come from me."

He answered, "Okay, let's see what happens."

It worked, and I had no more problems after doing so the rest of my days at the school. The students now knew I meant business in the classroom. And the principal respected my guts to make such a decision as an idealistic, neophyte teacher who saw the light.

It was the only time I had to perform corporal punishment my entire career in education. Why…because I also learned how to play the role of a didactic dictator my plebe year in the profession. There's only room for one leader in the classroom, and that's the teacher.

Nearing the end of my tenure at the school, Peggy and I took three of my students to a Pitt wrestling dual meet. It was the first time they had ever witnessed a wrestling match, so I had to explain the rules throughout the competition. The kids really enjoyed it.

Ironically, when we returned to my car after the bout, some vandals broke into the car and took my typewriter. It reminded me of a quote I once heard – "No good deed goes unpunished."

When I left the school, the regular physical education teacher continued to have the same problems. The girls' "Phys. Ed." teacher, who I worked closely with at the school, called me to say what Mr. Kisick told the regular physical education instructor at a faculty meeting, "I had a little permanent-substitute teacher who could handle the kids. Why can't you!"

Nothing I learned in the teacher-education classroom compared to what I dealt with through practical experience in the "teaching trenches." I learned how important classroom control was to teaching students.

This was the beginning stages of developing my educational philosophy: Student discipline is a must in the classroom that all great teachers possess. I don't care how brilliant a teacher may be in his or her area of expertise. If he or she can't control the classroom, nothing will be learned. This is the gospel truth in every K-12 educational environment, be it urban or rural.

The significance of classroom discipline was an educational epiphany for me at the beginning of my career that I lived by until the day I retired.

• • •

CHAPTER SIX

The Move to Wheeling

"Adventure is the champagne of life."
                                    - G. K. Chesterton

With a bit of experience and a sound educational philosophy, I completed my master's program in August of 1970. I had already applied to a number of school districts, including my hometown in which there was a teaching and head wrestling coach position open.

I thought, "Wouldn't it be great to teach and coach at my high school alma mater?"

It was not to be.

The school superintendent at the time was my high school principal. I guess he remembered what I was like in high school, particularly my senior year. Somehow he lost my application.

I was disappointed and frustrated, but my OCD would not allow me to give up on my quest to succeed as an educator, so I kept focused and kept applying.

I was offered a number of other teaching and coaching positions from some Pennsylvania schools and one in Wheeling, West Virginia. I chose Wheeling and the Ohio County Schools System because there I would have the opportunity to develop my own wrestling program as head coach.

So off we went to the Mountain State with the help of Rich Carter (already introduced to you). Rich and I became close in high school. In fact, I was the best man at his wedding.

• • •

At Ohio County Schools, I accepted a position at Edgington Lane Elementary School as a self-contained fourth and fifth grade teacher, along with my head wrestling coach position at Wheeling High School in the fall of 1970.

At Edgington Lane, I had the great privilege to meet and observe a true master teacher – Lynn Holderman. She taught me so much. We hit it off from the very beginning because like her, I believed in classroom control. The principal, Odessa Broemson, and I also got along well.

I really enjoyed teaching the fourth and fifth graders at the school. They actually walked (no running) into my classroom and stood at attention until I told them to take their seats.

Of course, I had to tone down my discipline practices a couple notches because the educational climate was more tamed and focused on academics. And since my first-year experience in Pittsburgh, as I previously mentioned, corporal punishment was no longer a part of my teaching repertoire.

My fifth graders were well-behaved kids who only heard about paddling from their parents. They actually asked me to paddle them so they could tell others they received corporal punishment. I obliged their request with a soft ping pong paddle whack on their butts.

They loved it and to this very day they tell me how much they appreciated the honor.

• • •

I really enjoyed having fun with my fourth and fifth grade reading classes at Edgington Lane. When studying silent letters in words, I would trick them with the following pseudo-phonics statement:

"Students, never forget the silent 'P' in swimming."

I always relished the look in their eyes as some of them figured it out, while others had totally confused expressions on their young faces.

It was precious to observe.

. . .

I was also the safety patrol sponsor. In this capacity, I instructed the students to march to and from their posts each day. The Wheeling Police officer in charge of overseeing all safety patrols in the county was so impressed with our patrol unit that he chose us as the best. My kids received a trophy for their efforts, and I treated them to a party in my classroom at the end of the school year.

. . .

As Wheeling High School's wrestling coach, my athletic director was Elmer Freese. He was a wonderful role model and a man I deeply respected to this very day. Mr. Freese introduced me to the school's administration and gave me a brief history of the school's many traditions in athletics as the Wheeling "Wildcats."

At wrestling practice, I had to deal with a diversity of students on the team. They came from all walks of life. I learned as much from them as they did from me. I made it my goal to understand and respect my athletes and the challenges they were up against. I was going to sprint the extra mile for each and every one of my wrestlers no matter their ability level.

One of my "Wildcat" wrestlers was Dave Iverson, who I made it my personal mission to guide him in the right direction. He was an outstanding competitor on the mats – when he showed up for practices and meets. I didn't kick him off the team for these indiscretions because I knew he came from a very dysfunctional family environment.

Since he often had problems making weight, I had him stay at our house one night to show him the proper dietary foods to eat. As Dave played with Billy and held our baby son, Ricky, Peggy prepared him a typical wrestler's meal – grilled chicken on toast, a salad accompanied with light dressing, fruit cocktail, tea, and a Hershey bar for dessert. Dave ate it with gusto.

After eating, we all went into the family room to watch television. But to my chagrin, he lit up a non-filtered Pall Mall. He thought nothing of it. I let it go: Wrestling is what kept Dave coming to school, as well as keeping him out of trouble in his crime-ridden surroundings.

The day Dave Iverson graduated from Wheeling High School, Peggy and I were there to witness his personal accomplishment.

Today, Dave is a very productive citizen in society.

• • •

On another occasion, before weigh-ins at a local tournament, one of my wrestlers, Frank Constantini was a few ounces over weight. He had long hair, but not after I borrowed a pair of trainer scissors. Frank made weight and he acquired a nickname that has stuck with him to this day.

If you see him, just holler, "Hi Nubs."

• • •

Being a young over-zealous coach at the time, I did make a terrible mistake for which I have to live with forever.

John Defelice was one of my lightweight wrestlers at Wheeling High. He was a great kid. One day at practice, he started complaining about his leg. I thought John was just tired and trying to get a break. So I made him continue wrestling.

Three hours later, I was visiting him with a box of candy at the hospital. John had a broken leg. His parents were there when I entered the room. They didn't blame me at all since they knew how much I cared about everyone of my "Wildcat" wrestlers.

But I felt bad; I should have listened to John at practice.

Since then, when my wrestlers complained to me about an ailment, I listened to them and checked out their physical concern before I let them continue to practice.

I learned my lesson.

• • •

I wasn't the only one fiercely loyal to the Wheeling High wrestling team. At one home match the official had to stop the competition because two females were shoving each other in the gym's balcony. It seems that one of the girls kept bad-mouthing me and my "Wildcat" wrestlers.

The next day Harold Blaney, the principal of the Wheeling High School, called me into his office. He requested that I talk to my wife Peggy, and explain to her that it is inappropriate for ladies pushing and shoving each other during a scholastic event. I was a little embarrassed and so was Peggy, but she said that she was only defending my honor.

How could I be upset with her?

. . .

It's uncanny, but coaches in all sports never forget their first squads. The same was true for me. Of the many championship teams I coached in dual meet and tournament competition, my most memorable win involved my Wheeling "Wildcats."

In January of 1972, we had a Saturday away meet with Warwood High School, a small school wrestling powerhouse in the area. They were coached by Dick Edge, a legendary mat mentor who initiated several wrestling programs in the upper Ohio Valley.

Clearly, my mat squad was in no way expected to prevail in the meet. At that time, my assistant coach Eric Carder and I thought differently. During my pre-meet talk, I simply said, "Boys, it's time to win a big one. We are wrestling our inter-city rivals who think they're going to kick our butts. You've worked damn hard at practice for two years; let's prove them and the news media wrong."

After our team prayer, my Wildcats were ready to pour out their souls on the mat.

I felt the magic in the air that day when Steve Hill, one of the finest black wrestlers I ever coached, lost a hard fought match, losing a close decision to John Vdovjak, a two-time state champ.

Even though we gained victories from Rick Fenimore, Jeff Richardson, Bill Taggart, Jim Greenwood, and Donnie Stewart, the Warwood "Vikings" were decisively winning the dual meet 30 to 19 with only two matches left.

At the 185-pound weight class, we had Jay Myers, a senior who was very light for that weight category. Warwood's grappler was an experienced 185-pounder with lots of varsity matches to his credit.

On the referee's whistle, Jay was immediately taken down and forced to his back. Coach Carder and I sighed, preparing for the inevitable slap of the mat by the official.

What we and everyone else present then witnessed was determination rarely seen in an athlete of any sport. For the entire first period, Jay Myers bridged off his back and avoided being pinned. His individual doggedness was nothing less than amazing.

Still, at the start of the second period, Jay was losing 5 to nothing.

For two years, I tried to break Jay Myers of what I considered a bad habit regarding a basic move, the side roll, from the bottom position. Performed properly, the reversal maneuver is negotiated from the knees. Jay devised a way of hitting the move on his stomach, locking his opponent's leg with his own and rolling the top wrestler over to his back.

His opponent had the choice the second period and selected the top position. Jay looked at me and smiled. We were the only two in the gym who understood the meaning of that grin. He executed his signature move, rolling his Warwood adversary to his back.

A few seconds later the official slapped the mat.

What a comeback!

Everybody in the facility was stunned, except Jay and me. I hugged Jay with sincere admiration when he came off the mat.

What incredible guts!

The score before the final heavyweight match of the inter-city dual meet was Warwood 30 and Wheeling 25.

Our heavyweight was Tim Wrixon. Although Tim weighed in excess of 300 pounds, he was exceptionally agile for a big man.

When the official started the match, Tim quickly locked his hands around the Warwood wrestler's back, securing a bearhug. Moments later, Wrixon lifted his opponent up, kicked his feet out from under him, slamming the Viking to his back.

With over a minute left in the first period, Tim score another six-point fall.

The house went suddenly silent as the Warwood contingency came to the realization that their team just lost the meet. In contrast, we were overjoyed with this surprising upset.

The final tally: Wheeling 31 Warwood 30

Some say wrestling is not a team sport. Well, I disagree. My Wheeling "Wildcats" demonstrated that the whole is greater than the sum of its parts that day on the mat.

• • •

You'll like this final note regarding my Wheeling High wrestlers. A few years after they graduated we had a team reunion. It was during this get-together that my "Wildcats" had a confession to make.

"Coach, remember when we shared Jeff Richardson's cool aid after weigh-ins and before each match."

"I do. And I often mentioned to Peggy how you guys took care of one another at practice and during matches. It made me proud to be your coach, whether you won or lost."

"Coach, that wasn't cool aid."

"What do you mean?"

"Coach, it was wine."

Shaking my head with a smile on my face, I said: "Now I know why you guys seemed so loose when competing."

I will never forget my "Wheeling High Boys."

• • •

The late Coach Mal Paul (Left) and the late Coach Lyman "Beans" Weaver of Shamokin High School were Bill Welker's coaches as a "Greyhound" wrestler. These men knew the significance of drill work for producing championship teams and wrestlers. As mat mentors, they not only developed winning athletes, but also molded boys into men, epitomizing the essence of integrity, hard work, and perseverance. Coach Paul and Coach Weaver have since been inducted into the National Wrestling Hall of Fame (Pennsylvania Chapter) and the Pennsylvania Wrestling Hall of Fame.

The names "Welker," "Shamokin," "state champion" began with Harold Welker. He won his title in 1938 during the first-ever Pennsylvania State Wrestling Championships held in "Rec Hall" at Penn State University.

Floyd Welker was crowned a Pennsylvania state wrestling champ in1959 and was a state runner-up his senior year at Penn State's "Rec Hall."

Bill Welker receiving his 1963 Pennsylvania State Wrestling Championship trophy from Dr. Eric A. Walker, president of Penn State University, upon defeating Sherm Hostler of Newport by a score of 4-2 at "Rec Hall."

Bill Welker, riding Dana Luckenbaugh of West York in the Pennsylvania state finals his senior year, was defeated by a narrow 4-3 margin at "Rec Hall." Bill ended his scholastic wrestling career with 83 victories and was old Shamokin High School's winningest wrestler. He was the last wrestler to compete in a "Greyhound" uniform. Bill and Floyd Welker were the first brother-team to win state championships in District Four, a hotbed of Pennsylvania wrestling.

Bill Welker and two-time Olympian Bobby Douglas pictured during the Ron Mauck Ohio Valley Athletic Conference Wrestling Championships. It was held at the Wesbanco Arena in Wheeling, West Virginia. Welker and Douglas, who is a Distinguished Member of the National Wrestling Hall of Fame, conducted numerous wrestling clinics together in West Virginia and Pennsylvania. Douglas wrote the forward for Bill Welker's *The Wrestling Drill Book*, which is a national best-seller.

Jack Aylor (Left), Director of Development for the College of Education and Human Services, inducts Dr. Bill Welker into West Virginia University's prestigious Jasper N. Deahl Honors Society for his contributions to education. The induction ceremony took place at the Ohio County Schools Board of Education meeting in Wheeling, West Virginia. Welker is the first educator from the school system to receive this professional award from the University.

Who says wrestlers with cauliflower ears don't attract the cutest girls? Bill Welker and his wife Peggy have experienced many mountains and valleys throughout their marriage. But with mutual goals, endurance and a partnership of love, Bill and Peggy raised four wonderful children on Wheeling Island in Wheeling, West Virginia. They are now enjoying their retirement and 15 grandchildren.

As the radio co-host on *The Rick Welker Wrestling Show* in Wheeling, West Virginia, Bill Welker has fun bantering with his son Rick for an hour every week during wrestling season. They discuss all facets of the mat sport, feature area and national wrestling personalities, and answer questions or listen to wrestling stories from callers. A regular on the show is Scott Jackson. He keeps the listeners up-to-date on team scores and matches to follow.

CHAPTER SEVEN

Wheeling Central High: A Time of Struggle

"The bravest sight in the world is to see a man struggle against adversity."

- Seneca

In February of 1972: During my second year as an elementary teacher in Ohio County, my wife and I were able to purchase our home on Wheeling Island. That's when things fell apart professionally.

I was informed in March that I was being RIF'd, which means the school system was having a "Reduction-In-Force" episode where new and non-tenured teachers' contracts were not renewed. At the end of the school year, I would be out of a job.

When it rains, it pours was not a figure of speech for the Welkers in June of 1972. We witnessed our first flood on Wheeling Island and were awe-struck, having no idea what to do being new to the neighborhood. There were actually boats maneuvering down our street.

The first half of 1972 was a dire time my wife and I would like to put out of our minds. But it was Peggy who kept the faith, knowing I was quite depressed at this point in my young teaching career. She was my strength when I really needed her support. You have to understand that we had no family and few friends in the Wheeling area.

It was a very scary period in our lives.

. . .

But in July, I received a phone call from Bill McEldowney, director of the Wheeling YMCA, where my "Wildcat" wrestlers practiced, came to our aid. He cared about our plight. Kindness comes in many different forms; Mr. McEldowney was made of such wonderful stuff.

He had contacted Nick Mansuetto, the athletic director at Wheeling Central High School, setting up an interview with Mr. Mansuetto on my behalf. The interview went great and I was hired by Central's iconic principal, Dr. Joseph Viglietta, as a reading and English teacher and head wrestling coach.

It is a small catholic institution comprised of energetic students and a dedicated professional staff who promoted an atmosphere of positive school spirit in the classroom and on the playing field.

. . .

While life was still a struggle, I was thankful to have a job – and as always, I managed to find fun and humor no matter the circumstances.

I always decorated a Christmas tree in the classroom behind my desk. One day as class was in session, I was rocking in my swivel chair when I flipped backwards, crashing into the tree.

There was total silence in the room as I nonchalantly set up the tree again.

Sitting back down, I calmly stated, "Okay, students, now where were we?"

The classroom exploded with laughter.

Then there was the time I was standing in front of the teacher's desk, lecturing to my English 12 students. While I was speaking, a male student, DJ Manners, sitting in the front muttered, "Mr. Welker."

"Get quiet, DJ."

"Mr. Welker."

"Shut up, DJ," I grumbled.

"But, Mr. Welker."

"What, DJ!"

He stood up, walked over to me and whispered in my ear, "Your zipper's down."

I turned around, adjusted my zipper, thanked DJ, and continued my lecture just a bit embarrassed.

There were a few snickers.

. . .

I enjoyed working with the students in the classroom and the wrestlers on the mats. My first season there, I produced a West Virginia state champion, Dan Doyle, in the winter of 1973. He was the second wrestler in the school's athletic history to do so. Dan was also the youngest and first member of a traditional Central wrestling family to do so.

Upon graduating from college, Dan Doyle gave back to the sport all it did for him. He became an outstanding wrestling coach in the Ohio Valley. Dan Doyle later acquired a doctorate in education prior to retiring as an exemplary coach, teacher and school administrator.

. . .

In the spring of my initial year at Wheeling Central, I received a surprise letter from an eastern college. I was invited to be interviewed for the positions of physical education instructor and head wrestling coach at York College, a small institution of higher learning in York, Pennsylvania.

At that time, I dreamed of becoming a college coach. Also, it would bring us closer to our Pennsylvania hometown.

What a deal!

I went for the day-long interview with the athletic director of the school on a Wednesday. The campus was beautiful. After returning to Wheeling Island, I received a phone call from the AD that night, offering me the job. I was elated, and so was Peg. We were going back home.

But then the bottom dropped out.

Late that Friday night, I received another call from the AD. As it turned out, he did recommend me for the position, but the president of York College wanted to hire another applicant who was a good friend of his during their college days. The AD told me how bad he felt and it took him hours to make the call.

I was crushed and cried in my wife's arms. She was just as sorrowful over the injustice, especially since she had two brothers and a sister who lived in the York area. Peggy would have loved living near them.

I couldn't understand why God ignored my prayers for such a position. It was as though He turned his back on me. I was depressed for weeks. I felt betrayed and I didn't know how to move forward.

Decades later, I realized that God had a plan for me that would be to my family's best interest. And I was reminded of a quote from Kirk Douglas when he found religion. A friend told him that God doesn't answer all prayers. Mr. Douglas retorted, "Oh, yes He does, but sometimes the answer is no."

There was one very bright spot in 1973; our beautiful daughter, Tiffany, was born in May.

．　．　．

I continued to teach reading and English classes and coached wrestling at Wheeling Central for the next three years. I was blessed with many fine athletes that I must mention: John and Pat Dolan, Tim and Rich Emmerth, Dave and Steve Camilletti, and Bernie Shalvey, who later played college football for Penn State legend, Joe Paterno.

．　．　．

While coaching at Central, I was amazed regarding the logic of two referees who I had to deal with during the rigors of competition.

The first encounter concerned a semi-final match in our 40-team conference tournament involving my 185-pounder, Steve Wojcik.

Steve's bout ended in a draw (1-1) after the regular match periods. When the minute's rest concluded, the next three one-minute overtime periods would determine the winner.

In the standing position the first period, neither wrestler was able to secure a takedown. Steve won the official's flip of the red-and-green disk and chose the bottom position in the second period. Upon the referee's whistle, Steve stood up and quickly procured an escape (2-1). Neither wrestler was able to score the rest of the second stanza.

Before the start of third period, Steve's opponent also chose the bottom position. As soon as the official started the final period, the other wrestler also attempted a stand-up escape, but Steve brought him down to the mat a few seconds later. The mat man continued to stand up numerous times during the period, finally earning an escape a few seconds before the match ended.

With the score 2-2, it was up to the referee to decide the winner.

I was fairly confident that Steve out-wrestled his opponent before the official's decision. To my shock, the referee raised Steve's opponent's hand. I immediately went to the score table for a conference with the official regarding his criteria for the choice he made.

"Sir, what was the basis for your decision?"

"Well, coach, the other boy made more attempts trying to escape during the third overtime period."

"That's because my wrestler quickly escaped on the first attempt at the start of the second overtime period. And furthermore, he held his opponent down much longer in the third period. What you're telling me is that I should have told my boy to fake stand-ups, and not to escape until the end of second period. Your decision makes no sense."

The referee finally replied, "Coach, you have a legitimate point, however, I saw it differently," as he walked away.

I was speechless.

But it was trivial compared to what I experienced my final year coaching at Central. The second incident on the mats has perplexed me for years. It occurred at the 1976 West Virginia State Wrestling Tournament held in Fairmont, West Virginia.

My Central heavyweight, Wayne Lichwa, wrestled his way to the state semi-finals. In the third period of the match, Wayne and his opponent were in the neutral position. As all big wrestlers do, Lichwa and his adversary were aggressively pummeling for the inside arm position.

Unfortunately, the referee in the bout misinterpreted their actions as fighting and disqualified both wrestlers.

I was completely dismayed, especially having observed the official in previous matches during the tourney. He seemed to perform competently, but he either panicked or over-reacted in this match.

I totally lost it.

Even other officials, who witnessed the match, attempted to persuade the official to overturn his call. But he finally stood by his decision. And I, well I was spitting nails and had to be removed from the gym. To make matters worse, this same referee was in the hospitality room when I entered. I lost it, again.

Needless to say, I was asked to leave there as well. I ate the sandwich I made inside my car.

I was not a happy camper.

There are a few other points you need to know to understand my rage. First, it was a rough season for Central wrestling and Wayne Lichwa was my only shining star. Second, the match was terminated with only 45 seconds left, and Wayne was winning by a score of 7 to 1.

Furthermore, his opponent actually told the referee to just disqualify him (if he had to disqualify anybody), and give Wayne the match because he knew he was beaten.

The worst part of it all, Wayne Lichwa would have competed in the state finals against a wrestler he beat the previous weekend at regionals. As it was, he got nothing and I was livid.

I must admit: If it had happened today, I would still be out in the parking lot eating a sandwich in my car.

As for me, I have made peace with the official in question. I wish I could say the same for Wayne.

My deepest regret is how it affected Wayne Lichwa. He still has sour feelings when it comes to officials in all sports.

As his coach, I can understand Wayne's feelings of bitterness.

• • •

The refs weren't the only ones making mistakes.

There is one home dual meet where I had to definitely agree with an official's call. My Wheeling Central wrestlers were pitted against Triadelphia High School. It was predicted to be a very close match.

I hired a veteran local official, Paul Lemery, well known in wrestling circles as a very competent judge of the mats.

It was during a close match in a middle weight class when Mr. Lemery made a very difficult call that went against my Central "Maroon Knight" wrestler. I was irate and yelled at Paul, "Bullshit!"

The problem is that my expletive resonated throughout the entire gym. Mr. Lemery looked at me, shrugged his shoulders, and hit me with an unsportsmanlike conduct team-point deduction.

I cowered and sheepishly sat back down in my coaching chair, realizing how important even a one-point forfeiture was to the final outcome of the meet. I may have cost my boys the match.

As it turned out, our heavyweight scored a fall in the third period. We won by one point.

Sheez.

• • •

While working at Central, family finances were very tight. I repeatedly had to request $50.00 advances in pay from Principal Joseph Viglietta, and we always owed our local grocer money. Likewise, our monthly budget was so limited that at one point we almost lost our home. To boost our income, Peggy and I found evening positions as a waitress and bartender. I also worked as a gardener and roofer during the summer months.

I was even unable to upkeep the house. My boys (Billy and Ricky) and other urchins in the neighborhood played baseball in our yard. At one point, we had six broken windows I didn't even have enough money to fix. We just taped cardboards over them until I was able to save enough money to replace the broken windows.

To this day, I am very frugal with household finances, a by-product from those lean years.

• • •

Another concern was family health issues since we did not have the money to purchase medical insurance. But fortunately we had a wonderful medical bene-factor – Dr. George "Bunny" Naum. He treated our children and us for all our physical ailments without monetary compensation during my years at Central. My wife and I cannot thank Dr. Naum enough for his kindness and generosity.

The long-term stress wore me down. It was during this period in my life, I had a minor "nervous breakdown," having problems sleeping at night, wor-rying over our finances. This was the dark side of my OCD. But with the lov-ing support of Peggy and counseling sessions with a clinical psychologist, Dr. Dorothy Jones, I was able to combat my "anxiety and panic attacks." Though deeply depressed, I never missed a day of work.

Although my time at Central was very rewarding as a teacher and coach, I had to find more solid footing for my family's future.

• • •

CHAPTER EIGHT

My Return to the Public School Arena and the Pursuit of a Doctorate

> *"I will study and prepare myself ... and some day my chance will come."*
>
> - Abraham Lincoln

When I was offered a position to return to the Ohio County Schools System in the summer of 1976, I knew it was time to leave Central and move forward. But there was still a problem; I had to go back to undergraduate school to acquire nine credits in language arts.

I earned those hours at West Liberty State College (now West Liberty University) that summer, and in the fall I began teaching at Warwood Junior High School and coaching wrestling at the newly-consolidated Wheeling Park High School.

I need to thank Jim Monderine, the school's principal, and my former assistant at Wheeling High School, Eric Carder, who was then the head wrestling coach at Wheeling Park, for helping me to obtain these new positions.

•　　•　　•

I was designated as the head coach of the junior varsity and sophomore "Patriot" wrestlers for three years at Wheeling Park. This position was assigned to me by Coach Carder, who knew my expertise working with novice mat men.

We had our own room where I taught them the fundamentals of wrestling. In all sports, basics are a "must" for success.

I affectionately referred to these boys as my "Grubbers." My training included abundant drill work coupled with intense workouts. They loved and hated me simultaneously, but never doubted my ability to improve their talents as scholastic wrestlers.

My goal was to prepare them for the varsity room and competition at the next level. After leaving my room, many of the boys later had very successful careers in the varsity arena. A couple became state champs. It was a very rewarding experience as a coach.

One of my grubbers was Joe Thomas, a competitor who deeply loved the mat sport, but had very little athletic ability. Joe and I became best friends later in life. He owned a restaurant and lounge, The Harbor Lights, which I frequented often my last years as a teacher.

He traveled with me to many wrestling events which included the West Virginia State Wrestling Tournament and the Pittsburgh Wrestling Classic, where Pennsylvania All-Stars competed against great wrestlers from across the United States.

Joe Thomas also went with me and local official Ray Marling to my hometown, meeting my parents and high school wrestling coaches. At a get together hosted by my good friend, Ron Weller, Joe said to my coaches, "Bill has boasted he invented a pancake takedown from the knees," in a friendly attempt to call my bluff.

Coach Weaver replied, "Yes, Billy did."

I just smiled at Joe as he was at a loss for words.

Joe Thomas was engaged to his love Jeannie and planned a summer wedding. That was not to be. After selling his lounge and just beginning a new job, Joe had a massive heart attack and died instantly. Jeannie was heartbroken, and so was I.

My most endeared "Grubber" had passed.

I will never forget his friendship. In so many ways, Joe was my coach. He further taught me the importance of humility in life.

I loved him as a brother.

• • •

My fourth and final year as coach at Wheeling Park, I was assigned as "interim head coach" while Coach Carder finished his master's degree program.

I had the privilege to work with such wrestlers as Will and Brian Myers, Rusty and Greg Jewell, Frank McNeil, Barry Barbe, Jim Copney, Rodd Haller, Jim West and Sean O'Brien.

They say that sports test an individual's innate ethical values. In this new coaching position, the mettle of my character was tested at our conference wrestling championships.

George Stanley was my 112-pounder, a very physical wrestler. However, George was getting whipped the first two periods of his semi-finals bout. His opponent was a veteran wrestler by the name of McCormick from Union Local High School.

At the beginning of the third period, McCormick was in the down position. On the whistle, he quickly scored a stand-up escape, leading by a score of 6-1. Neither wrestler scored a takedown the majority of the period. Then with only 20 seconds left in the match, McCormick picked Stanley up and smashed him to the mat.

The official immediately stopped the match and penalized McCormick for an illegal slam. He was now leading by a score of 6-2, as George lay motionless on the mat and recovery time was started.

I now had to make a coaching decision on whether George Stanley should continue or not. I noticed that George was stunned, but not badly hurt.

As I was walking toward Stanley, I thought if I tell George to stay down, he would win the match due to the infraction … and George would be in the finals.

When I kneeled down by him, I said, "George, there are only seconds left in the match and you're losing by four points. It's time for our desperation move, the Lateral Drop (aka a Standing Pancake). Now get out there George and make it happen. I know you can do it."

McCormick's coach was also very knowledgeable and knew exactly what our tactics would be, saying to his wrestler, "There are only 20 seconds left; dance around and definitely do not tie up with him."

As soon as the official restarted the match, George shoved McCormick back, setting up the move, and he retaliated by driving into George.

Perfect.

George over- and under-hooked his adversary in the ideal Pancake position, throwing McCormick's back to the mat with his own momentum. When the buzzer sounded, the official awarded George two points for the takedown and three near-fall points, winning the match 7-6.

I have often thought about that match. What if I would have told George to take a "dive," what would I have been teaching him? Of course, the answer is … to cheat. I would have lost the respect of George and his fellow teammates.

To this very day, I thank the Lord for guiding me in making the right decision. Over my years of coaching, I was learning to make calm decisions that put my honor – and the honor of my team – first. As much as I wanted to win as a coach, I tried my best never to put winning before ethics.

•   •   •

George's older brother was Carl Stanley, the best wrestler I ever coached or witnessed on the upper Ohio Valley mats. He had mat sense second to none. During his scholastic career, Carl won three Ohio Valley Athletic Conference titles and two West Virginia state championships.

Like George, who was a West Virginia All-State wrestler, I also taught Carl my Pancake takedown series. Years after Carl graduated from high school, we were fooling around on the mats between sessions at an area youth tournament. Surprisingly, Carl took me down with my signature move, the Pancake. Although I was quite embarrassed, I was also pleased that Carl perfected the maneuver.

In essence, the student had become the master. And isn't that the goal of any good coach?

It was for me.

•   •   •

My initial years at Warwood Junior High School finances were still tight. I found myself playing catch-up with the bills that I accumulated during the Wheeling Central years. Still, I was able to set aside some money for my family to visit Mom and Dad in Shamokin for the Easter weekend. Our family had grown to six with the arrival of our third son, Dan-E.

When we left on Thursday morning, the weather was beautiful on the five-hour drive across Pennsylvania to Shamokin. Mom and Dad were excited about seeing their grandkids, especially our new addition to the family.

The visit was wonderful and, as always, it was hard to say good-bye Easter Sunday after church.

It was another sunny day when we started home.

After a couple of hours driving, we stopped at Dave's Dream, in the Hollidaysburg area, to enjoy a mid-afternoon meal. The diner also sold delicious homemade bread and pies. After purchasing raisin bread for Peggy upon leaving, I had ten dollars left in my wallet. But that was no problem because our next stop would be Wheeling.

As we passed Huntingdon, it started to snow lightly. But as we traveled further west, it turned into a blizzard. Nearing Ebensburg, I couldn't see ten feet in front of me as I slowly drove up a long incline.

At the top of the hill which is part of the eastern edge of the Allegheny Mountains, I realized we could go no further.

Fortunately, I knew that there was a motel close by. As we drove into the parking lot of The Cottage Inn, my car slid to a stop. We parked in front of the motel office.

I led the way as the family entered the motel. We had to get in line because others were also seeking shelter from the elements. When I approached the desk clerk, I realized I only had ten dollars to my name.

I explained to the clerk my family's predicament, and that I would send him a check on Monday when we reached home. I even went as far as to offer him my Pitt class ring as collateral.

He looked at Peggy and the kids and said, "I'm sorry, sir, but it costs $35.00 a room. Don't you have a credit card?"

"No, I don't."

"Then I can't help you."

"But what about my family?"

"I'm sorry, but that's your problem."

A man, who was right behind us, stepped forward and said, "Put his room fare on my credit card."

I didn't know what to say, but "Thank you so much; I'll send you a check Monday."

"I'm not worried about that; I didn't want your family sleeping in the car all night. My name's Dr. Miller; I'm a dentist in Greensburg."

"Well, Dr. Miller, Peggy and I can't thank you enough. What is your address?"

"Here's my business card."

I then introduced him to my family and told him that I was a teacher from Wheeling. He told us he had been there many times and wished us a safe trip the rest of the way home.

That Monday I sent a check to him and a "Letter to the Editor" of the Greensburg newspaper, expressing my gratitude to Dr. Miller.

I promised myself that I would do the same for a person in need someday in the future.

Since then, I fulfilled that commitment, a number of times.

•   •   •

While the years rolled on, life continued its ups and downs. Sometimes we found help from strangers like Dr. Miller, but more often my help came from someone much closer to home: Peggy. Nobody can question the intuition of a good mother, and Peggy is no exception.

It was during Dan-E.'s fourth grade year when my wife looked at me and said, "Dan-E.'s too small."

I said, "What?"

"Bill, our Dan-E. is too little for his age."

"Peggy, you and I are small and so are our kids."

"NO! I can tell; Dan-E. is too short even for a Welker," retorted my wife.

Knowing I wasn't going to win this argument, I scheduled an appointment for Dan-E. with our family doctor, George Naum.

At the doctor's office, I stood there in awe as Peggy explained to this veteran physician, "My boy is too little."

"Peggy, you and Bill are small in physical stature. You have to expect that your kids will be the same, too."

Peggy would not accept this answer and replied, "I do not mean to be disrespectful, Dr. Naum, but I feel strongly that Dan-E. is too short even for a Welker."

Even Dr. Naum couldn't change Peggy's mind.

Realizing he would not win this battle with a determined mother, Dr. Naum scheduled appointment for Dan-E. with a specialist involved with children's growth problems.

The outcome of that next visit was a surprise to everyone, but Peggy. We learned from the specialist that Dan-E. had a deformed pituitary gland, which was not secreting enough "growth hormone." The doctor immediately placed our youngest son on a synthetic growth hormone.

Had this abnormal condition gone undetected, our youngest son would have grown to be no taller than 4 feet and 11 inches as an adult.

Today, Dan-E. is over five-foot, seven inches tall. In fact, he is three inches taller than me. Since then, I have never questioned Peggy when she had maternal advice regarding our children.

. . .

Over the years, I fell in love with Warwood Junior High School, where I taught reading and language arts classes. The parents were very supportive and wanted only the best for their children. I initiated many reading incentive programs, including an innovative annual "Controlled Reading Tournament" at the school.

. . .

Several relationships with colleagues were very influential during my years at Warwood.

I always went to school early during my initial years at Warwood, usually around six in the morning. So did Sam DeFillippo, who was the first principal at the newly consolidated Wheeling Park High School.

He was nearing the end of his career and spent his final years teaching history at Warwood. We had many great morning discussions, and I always listened to his words of wisdom. One bit of advice he shared with me was: "If you want to know what's going on in the school, befriend the custodians. Treat them as equals and you will always have a clean classroom."

Mr. DeFillippo's classroom was next to mine and I could tell the kids really liked him. When he retired, I deeply missed his altruistic nature and professional companionship.

. . .

Another older teacher who had a profound effect on my philosophy of life was Pat Walling, the science teacher at Warwood Junior High School. When I had car problems those early years at Warwood, Mr. Walling would drive me to and from school.

We had many conversations in his car those days, or should I say that I was the student, listening to his views on having a fulfilling existence in this world.

One of his adages I will eternally remember was "Man can resist anything, but temptation."

It really hit home, remembering many of the temptations I succumbed to as a young college student.

I learned from his fatherly lectures.

.   .   .

After resigning from coaching at the high school in 1980, I then coached football, wrestling, and track at Warwood. I decided I wanted to spend much more time with the kids I taught in the classroom.

During this period of time, my wife obtained a position as a dental assistant in a pediatric dental office. This is the profession she trained for at Georgetown University in the Washington, DC area after graduating from high school.

Her work ethic as a dental caregiver has always been exceptional. She was highly respected, admired and loved by the parents and children she worked on over the next 30 years.

.   .   .

In the meantime, I was able to further my education. My goal was to receive certification as a reading specialist. It took me two years to earn this certificate at West Virginia University.

While working on my reading certification, I learned a traumatic, test-taking lesson in an educational psychology class I needed to take. It occurred during the final exam of the course.

My grade for the course was a solid "A." I was quite prepared to score the same on the final examination. Then I made a terrible blunder.

There was a section on the psychology examination with very explicit directions: "Place a check mark besides those statements that are not true in reference to the beliefs of B. F. Skinner."

I answered all the items with the utmost confidence, but to my surprise, I received a "B" on the final exam and in the course. I was very disappointed and requested a conference with the class professor.

It was during our review of my answers that I realized my fatal error. I carelessly misread the directions, omitting in my mind the word "not."

All my answers in that section of the final exam were wrong, thus the lower grade.

My psychology professor was very sympathetic, but it was too late to do anything about it.

After that negative academic experience, I have always taught my students to read test directions very carefully, so they would never make the same mistake.

Overall, it was great to be back in the graduate classroom again. The chairperson of the reading department at WVU, Dr. Marilyn Fairbanks, took me under her wing and suggested that I think about pursuing a doctorate in reading education.

After talking it over with my wife, I decided to become a doctoral candidate in the field of reading, with a minor in educational administration in the fall of 1985. It would further my chances for future promotions as well as increase my salary classification.

•   •   •

As you can expect, the mid to late 1980s was a busy time for me, working on my terminal degree.

At the same time, I also tutored area students of all grade levels with various reading disability problems on Saturday mornings. It helped with my gas money to and from Morgantown, West Virginia during my doctoral program of studies.

The trial-and-error strategies of private tutoring gave me even more ideas on how to improve my classroom students' reading abilities.

I was teaching full-time and coaching three sports as well as officiating wrestling and umpiring Pony League Baseball. It was a very hectic, but exciting, time in my life.

Though I was taking my studies very seriously, I still had time to laugh at myself. Each morning before school started, I ran in the gym. I had one very painful, but humorous, experience after running in early October of 1986. While putting on my boxer shorts, I was stung by a bee in a very sensitive part of my body; I'll leave where to your imagination.

My fellow teachers caught drift of this painful incident. Their response: On Halloween, the women teachers dressed up as bees and the male teachers were attired as beekeepers. There was even a photo of them in the local newspapers.

I was totally embarrassed!

•   •   •

After school each day, I would be coaching one sport or another and then drive 75 miles to Morgantown for doctoral classes three to four nights a week for nearly four years.

•   •   •

There were many hurdles to overcome during my doctoral studies. Before even starting classes, I had to score high enough on the Miller's Analogy Test to be invited to take classes. This I succeeded in accomplishing. Next, I had to put together my doctoral committee of five professors. After doing so, I met with the committee for the first time to determine my course of studies.

It was determined that I would have to take 23 courses (69 hours of credit), not including 15 more hours during the dissertation phase – a total of 84 hours to complete the terminal degree.

To share some further information, I had a master's degree plus 55 graduate hours prior to working on my doctor of education degree. Unfortunately, many of the past courses I took were too old to be accepted as part of my doctoral curriculum, so I had to take some of them over again. My point being, while most doctoral programs have an average of between 55 to 65 hours needed to complete the degree curriculum, my program of study was 84 hours. Thus, I was given no preferential treatment being a veteran teacher.

Even after my coursework was determined, I still was not a formal doctoral candidate. I had to successfully complete two semesters of courses as a full-time student.

Take note: While striving for a doctoral degree, the graduate student could not receive any grades below a "B." If you did, you would be required to retake the course.

Having scored all "A's" my first two semesters, I was formally accepted into the doctor of education program.

Another hurdle completed.

Throughout those years of class work, my most humbling experience was an advanced statistics course involving linear regression. There were times when I was so totally lost that I didn't even know what kind of questions to ask Professor Paterson. He was kind to me. I earned a "B" by the skin of my teeth. I couldn't thank him enough.

I would be remiss if I didn't mention one of my favorite professors – the late Dr. Steven Stahl. A Harvard graduate, he was a renowned expert on reading comprehension and vocabulary instruction. I had him for several courses and we became very good friends.

During many classroom sessions, I would often give Dr. Stahl a hard time. On more than one occasion, I would answer his questions with some wisecrack remarks. In retaliation, he would often throw an eraser at me, shouting, "Welker, you're a piece of work."

I deeply miss him.

My fourth and final year was totally devoted to developing a dissertation topic. I must admit that I had been developing a topic at the outset of my doctoral journey. Simply stated, I was working on a pre-reading "storytelling" strategy which would prepare the students for the key themes or concepts they would then learn about in their textbooks.

By the 1988 Christmas break, I completed the first three chapters in preparation for my next hurdle – the "Prospectus Meeting" with my doctoral committee.

At this gathering the committee first decides whether they will accept a research topic. They approved my project.

The Committee also recommends changes to be made prior to the final presentation known as the "Oral Defense of the Dissertation."

As for me, my dissertation topic was accepted with some minor changes and the "Defense" was set for May of 1989.

Now for the final hurdle.

On the morning of May 11, 1989, I faced the Committee and proceeded to defend my dissertation topic. Three hours later, after my presentation and answering tons of questions from committee members, I successfully defended my research paper with a few modifications I was required to make.

The last hurdle to the finish line was surpassed and I earned my doctor of education degree in reading at West Virginia University.

What a roller coaster ride!

You're more than welcome to read my doctoral research document, but I'm afraid you would fall asleep by the second page. Oh yes, it would be quite boring to the layman.

• • •

CHAPTER NINE

Family and Officiating: The Lighter Side of Life

"Life is a long lesson in humility."
                                    - Sir James M. Barrie

The decade of the 80's was not all work for me. Each August, Peggy and I took Ricky, Tiffany, and Dan-E. to Knoebel's Grove Amusement Park in Elysburg, Pennsylvania. Yes, it's the place where I attended many dances in high school.

It was great to finally enjoy some long overdue quality time with the family. Likewise, my mind was focused on fun activities and relaxation rather than on the mental, emotional, and physical rigors of my many activities during the school year.

The park is nestled in a valley between two evergreen-clad mountains, and a fresh water creek runs through it. It is a family-oriented resort in which no alcohol is allowed on the grounds. Ron "Buddy" Knoebel, along with other siblings, runs the park.

We became good friends in high school through wrestling. As a senior at Lycoming College in Williamsport, Pennsylvania, Buddy was a Division II national champion.

Peggy and I rented a cottage for two weeks in the middle of the park called the White Dove. Being only seven miles away from Shamokin, my parents were able to visit us often, delighting in homemade ice cream at day's end.

They were retired, healthy and enjoying life to the fullest. In the winter months, they traveled south to Florida.

Our three youngest children loved it there and befriended the local high school and college students who operated many of the rides during the summer months. In turn, these young workers would let them on the rides free of charge, especially our youngest son, Dan-E. He spent the whole day either on the rides or swimming in the park's outdoor heated pool.

When they weren't running around the park, swimming or playing the arcade games, Ricky and Tiffany procured part-time jobs at the park, collecting ride tickets. They enjoyed the extra spending money.

How did they get hired in such short notice? It pays to know the boss.

Our oldest son, Billy, stayed home while in high school because he was a pitcher on a local baseball team that competed all summer long. He also played shortstop or second base when he wasn't on the mound. Although Billy was a three-time, all-state wrestler, his athletic love has always been baseball.

While we were away, Billy's singular responsibility was to care for the security of our home. And for a number of summers he did an excellent job, but like all teenage boys, Peggy and I knew we would have some cleaning up to do when the rest of the family returned home.

That changed dramatically the summer between Billy's junior and senior years. After another wonderful time at Knoebel's, we were astonished when we entered the house. It smelled like Pine Sol and the whole domain was in immaculate condition.

At first, we were very impressed with Billy's housekeeping abilities. Later in the day, however, I learned why he was so fastidious in his household duties.

Two days before we arrived home, Billy decided to have a small party with a couple of his baseball buddies. Well, each of his friends invited others, and so on. The party expanded to over 75 guests (boys and girls), who were drinking beer and making such a racket that our neighbors called the police.

The officers arrived, broke up the festivities, sending all the underage drinkers on their way. Billy was finally questioned as to the whereabouts of his parents.

It got even worse when the local Wheeling television station caught wind of the imbibing teenage gathering. It spotlighted the teenage drinking incident on the nightly news.

The major themes of the broadcast were: "Where were the parents? Should the parents be responsible for their children's illegal activities?"

They even videotaped the front of our house. Peggy and I were abundantly embarrassed, and for a few days, afraid to show our faces in public, especially me being a local educator.

At least, our names were not mentioned.

Of course, Peggy and I took punitive action. Billy was grounded for the rest of the summer.

There was one positive outcome regarding the matter. A month after the police raid, the Wheeling City Council passed a proclamation in which there was a 10 p.m. community curfew for teens under the age of eighteen.

Remembering my juvenile transgressions, Peggy jabbed, "The apple doesn't fall far from the tree."

As always, whenever one of our children got into trouble of one kind or another, the blame ultimately ended up on my lap.

So be it.

· · ·

My work was my work, my family was my joy—and as always, sports were my treasured hobby. I'd now gone from player to coaching and officiating. In all areas, what I love most about each sport is in the details. As a wrestling and baseball official, I always prided myself in being consistent— even to a fault.

· · ·

Speaking of my avocation as a sports official, I would like to share with you some unusual situations that occurred under my jurisdiction.

In this capacity as an athletic overseer, I always attempted to be as fair as possible. But I have to tell you about some interesting situations I had to deal with in both sports.

· · ·

I have officiated 100s of wrestling tournaments and dual meets over three decades. Furthermore, athletic organizations at the local, state, regional, and national levels have praised my work with numerous awards. Though I have always appreciated their support, what I remember the most are the blunders

I have made over the years as a mat sport arbiter. There were three grievous errors which embarrassed me the most.

The Saturday afternoon sessions of wrestling tournaments are quite tiring for officials because they're the longest of the event.

One such afternoon, I had been officiating for nearly three hours. I just started the first period of a match with the wrestlers in the standing position. As the one wrestler shot a double-leg tackle, his opponent legally wrapped his arms around the aggressor's head.

At that moment, I had what we in the officiating ranks refer to as a "brain fart." Due to fatigue, I was so fixated on the head lock that I didn't realize the aggressor secured a takedown before they spun out of bounds.

I missed the takedown completely, and it was too late to award points. As we walked back to the center of the mat, the coach, whose wrestler did not score the takedown, was standing by the scorer's table.

Appearing extremely agitated, he understandingly motioned me over for a conference.

Slowly working my way to the scorer's table, I thought, "What in the world am I going to tell this coach?"

He angrily inquired, "Welker, can you explain to me why my boy didn't earn a takedown?"

"No coach; I can't. I blew it. For some reason, I got distracted and lost my concentration on the match. I have no excuse; I just blew the call."

"Well, okay Bill. But make sure it doesn't happen again."

"You can count on it, coach."

Sometimes it's best that officials admit their mistakes. Had I tried to bluff my way out of the situation, the coach would have become even more upset, knowing I was attempting to cover up my oversight.

By my admission, I avoided a heated verbal confrontation with the coach. It also appeased the coach: How can one argue when both are in agreement?

As an official, honesty is always the best approach, and most coaches do appreciate it, even when you mess up.

• • •

On another occasion, I was officiating a one-day tournament at Shadyside, Ohio, where the fans from two schools (Shadyside and Bridgeport) were at each others' throats throughout the entire event.

It so happened that I was assigned to officiate the 171-pound finals match in which the participants were from the two schools mentioned above.

Furthermore, the bout would determine which school would win the competition.

The first two periods of the championship match went as smooth as an official could ever want, without any questionable or tough calls. I wish I could say the same for the third period.

The wrestler whose choice it was at the start of the third period selected the top position.

At the whistle, the wrestlers maneuvered into a tangled position on the mat. Without realizing it, the top wrestler locked hands around the bottom mat man's body, which is a one-point technical violation that is awarded to the opponent.

As soon as I hand-gestured the infraction while kneeling on the mat, the bottom man quickly switched his opponent and placed him on has back. Then his adversary reversed him, placing him on his back as well. The flurry of moves continued until the end of the period with the match ending in a tie, 14-14.

As mentioned in a previous chapter, if the bout ended in a draw, the wrestlers would get a minute's rest and then wrestle three one-minute periods, unless a wrestler was pinned anytime during the overtime action.

It was about 15 seconds into the rest period when my assistant (Jim Crosier) asked, "Bill, did you indicate locked hands?"

"Yep."

"Did you award the point?"

"Nope."

"Are you going to, Bill?"

"No, I'm going to eat the point, Jim. If I award it now, all hell would break lose in the gym. Remember, the Shadyside and Bridgeport fans have been screaming at each other all day long. Awarding the point now would cause a riot in the house. We'll let the match play itself out and pray the right wrestler wins."

"Okay, Bill, it's your call."

Thank God, at the conclusion of the bout the correct wrestler did, in fact, come out the victor.

In essence, although I made an incorrect decision, I did it for a righteous reason, the safety of all in attendance.

•   •   •

Every sport has its problem areas when it comes to official judgment calls – in baseball it is the strike zone, in football it is holding, and in wrestling it is the stalling penalty.

As for stalling, I was conservative, which means I indicated stalling less frequently than some other officials. Whether the coaches liked it or not, they always knew what to expect from me. Coaches don't like surprises.

The following narrative demonstrates a unique stalling call I made in a wrestling match.

It was in the finals of a holiday wrestling tournament a number of years ago that I was never as sure of a wrestler stalling as I was that night. The wrestlers were in the neutral position when Wrestler A shot a double leg, and Wrestler B countered and spun behind for the takedown.

At this point, Wrestler A decided to stall. In fact, he placed himself in a fetal-like position. Being an official who was more conservative with his stalling calls, I gave Wrestler A some time to readjust and start moving.

He never did.

For once, in my three decades as an official, I was absolutely sure of the stalling call I was about to make. With all the confidence of my many years of wrestling experience, I thrust my fisted hand in the air (indicating stalling), expecting no complaints from anybody in the gym.

Well, I was absolutely wrong. Wrestler A's coach came running out on the mat screaming at me. I was about to kick him out of the facility when he angrily informed me that his wrestler was knocked out.

And so he was.

Apparently, the only two people that did not know the boy was comatose were yours truly and my assistant referee, whose name I will withhold to protect his officiating reputation.

Totally embarrassed, I immediately informed the scorekeeper to erase the warning for stalling.

A coach once told me, "Welker, unless a wrestler is unconscious, you won't call stalling."

I suppose he was right.

• • •

I always enjoyed officiating and sometimes listening to wrestlers' cute comments during a match.

For over 30 years, I authored a column on Ohio Valley wrestling entitled "Mat Talk." As I was officiating one tournament match, I received a left-handed compliment from a wrestler.

He shot a number of takedowns near the out-of-bounds line, finishing the move outside the wrestling area. Thus, he was unable to score takedown points on each of his attempts.

As we were walking back to the center of the mat after one such takedown failure, he said to me, "Mr. Welker, I really enjoy your wrestling articles in the newspaper. Why don't you just stick to writing and forget officiating?"

He smiled and I laughed.

I was very impressed with the young wrestler's quick-witted statement. And as I raised his hand at the end of the bout, I told him that I would seriously consider his advice.

Years later, he and I joked about his youthful statement regarding my officiating abilities as he was being honored as a past championship wrestler in our local conference.

• • •

One of the most vocal coaches I ever worked for in the upper Ohio Valley was Dave LaMotte. He was a 1979 NAIA National Champion who coached the Bridgeport High School "Bulldogs" to an Ohio State Championship in 1988.

I will never forget the first dual meet I officiated for Coach LaMotte. It was a close match in which the Bulldogs finally prevailed.

After the competition, Coach LaMotte cornered me in the official's locker room. LaMotte was upset with a call I made during a middle weight bout.

"Welker, that was the worst stalling call I have ever seen!"

"But coach, your boy was just hanging on the lower leg, not attempting to improve his position on top."

"That's because his opponent was pushing his head down; you really blew that call!"

"Coach LaMotte, I have another Bridgeport dual meet next week for you. If you would rather have someone else for the match, I will completely understand."

"Heck no, Bill! You're one of the best referees in the valley. Don't forget weigh-ins are at 6:00 p.m. See you then."

As he walked away, I smiled while scratching my head.

• • •

I rarely refereed youth wrestling tournaments.

They say the more things change, the more things stay the same. Remember the negative experience I witnessed as a boy in Little League regarding parent-coaches over 50 years ago. Well, as I am sure you know, the same overzealous athletic parents still exist today in sports, including wrestling.

Against my better judgment, I have, on occasion, succumbed to the pleas of a friend to officiate at youth competitions. And as a veteran official, I assumed the position of head referee. The parental horror stories continue.

At one youth competition, a beginning official ejected an irate coach. After the decision, the tournament director suggested that he was going send the young official home because he didn't agree with the call. Of course, the coach, who was removed, happened to be the director's buddy.

I politely informed the director that if he did so, the rest of us would follow the young official out the door. That problem was settled.

At another small-fry event, I was officiating a match in which there were no close calls. All of a sudden, the father-coach at the corner went berserk. I had no idea what set him off as I kicked him out of the tournament.

Later, the tournament director asked, "Bill, if the coach just coaches his kids on the other mats, would that be okay?"

"No. He must leave the facility. If not, I'm leaving."

My advice to new officials is to start at the junior high level – where coaches are required to behave in an appropriate manner – to gain sufficient confidence before overseeing youth tournaments. Too many beginning referees have been chased out of the sport by self-serving, parent-coaches who rarely know many rules at the youth level.

No need to say more.

• • •

As a baseball umpire, I called low strikes and was pretty much a "pitcher's umpire." Anything close, you had better be swinging. Again, all the coaches knew what to expect from me behind the plate.

One particular incident on the diamond a coach questioned my ability as an umpire during a seven-inning game.

It was right before the top of the seventh inning when he kiddingly shouted at me: "Welker, you've been terrible for six innings; don't get good on me in the seventh!"

I didn't. Now that's consistency.

．　　●　　●

I don't know if small-fry wrestling, Little League baseball or other youth sports build or reveal character, but I do believe in the innocence of children. And my belief was reaffirmed at one summer Bronco baseball game many years ago. The players at this level are 11 and 12 years of age.

I was the Umpire-in-Chief behind home plate during a tournament game when an 11-year old boy hit a pop-fly to right-center field. The base umpire was in the proper position to observe the play.

The center fielder and right fielder crossed past each other as the ball came down. Both the base umpire and I thought the right fielder caught the ball, but when we looked at the center fielder, he stood up with the ball in his right hand.

Did he catch it or not?

The base umpire called time and motioned me out to the infield to discuss the situation. Meanwhile, the batter was on first base and his first-base coach began screaming at me to make a decision.

Very calmly, I told the coach to relax, that everything would be straightened out in a fair manner.

He continued to loudly voice his opinion.

Finally, as the chief umpire, I made my decision. I told the base umpire to ask the center fielder if he caught the ball or picked it up. At this point, the coach went ballistic, screaming: "YOU CAN'T DO THAT!"

From there it was all down hill for him. The coach lost perspective and composure. Naturally, I had no choice but to remove him from the field of play.

Seconds later, the base umpire returned with the verdict. The young center fielder told him, "I picked the ball up from the ground."

If only the coach would have waited five seconds before vehemently protesting. Instead, his boy was safe at first and he was "thrown out" of the game.

Some of you may think I took a big chance with the decision I made. Well, I don't. As adults, who have witnessed more of the darker side of human nature, we often forget about the innocence of youth, especially kids who are 11 or 12.

Fortunately, I have worked with children of that age group for many years in which I have often observed their purity and intrinsic honesty in the classroom.

Isn't it a joy to know that real innocence is still alive and well — and found in our youth!

• • •

I have often been quoted as saying, "Always listen to the advice of the most experienced person because he has made the most mistakes."

Well, listen to the advice I am about to give you now.

Grandma Welker and yours truly were attending my grandson Nate's baseball game. He's our daughter Tiffany's child. By the time the game was due to begin, the umpire did not show up.

One of my grandson's coaches knew I was a veteran baseball official. He asked if I would arbitrate the game. How could I say no?

Big error in judgment!

The last inning of the game with two outs, my grandson, Nate, hit a line drive into center field. If he scored an inside-the-park homerun, the game would go into extra innings. As he rounded third base, the outfielder threw the ball to the third baseman. He, in turn, would have to throw a perfect shot to the catcher to get the runner out. He did, and I called my grandson out at home, ending the game.

It was absolutely the right call, but absolutely against the wrong kid.

When I made my decision, Peggy came running down the first base side, screaming at me, "How could you do that to your grandson!"

The opposing coaches were amazed as well when they heard I was Nate's grandfather.

As far as my family was concerned that night, I was most definitely a familial pariah.

A month later I asked Nate, "Who is your favorite umpire?"

He definitively stated, "Not you!"

Learn from my mistake if you want to have a happy home life.

• • •

CHAPTER TEN

My Thoughts on Teacher Meetings, Strikes,
Unions and Becoming an Administrator

"Try not to be a man of success, but rather a man of value."
                                                    - Albert Einstein

After receiving my doctorate, my teaching days were far from over. In fact, I was beginning the second half of my 40-year teaching career in the fall of 1989.

At the start of that first year as Dr. Welker, Ohio County Schools invited a gentleman by the name of Cantor, who developed the "Cantor Discipline Program," to come speak to all the teachers about how to better manage their classrooms.

It was designed to assist teachers who were having student behavior problems in the classroom.

Mr. Cantor put on a day-long presentation that I believe involved a five-step classroom discipline procedure that included a warning and multiple checkmarks. I was amused.

When his program was over, I walked into the assistant principal's office, and looked at Mr. Ray Chenoweth with a smile on my face.

He smiled back and said, "Bill, you just keep on doing what you do regarding your classroom discipline practices."

"I plan to."

It has always been my experience and belief that teachers either have the innate skill to control their students or completely lack the ability. With such teachers, student-disruptions are a daily occurrence in their classrooms. And unfortunately, outside assistance on classroom management has rarely helped to improve their discipline problems.

Frankly stated, they lack the strength of character to present themselves as authority figures in front of their students. And without the respect of their students, they will forever experience classroom chaos.

• • •

Over the years, I have attended dozens of educational workshops conducted by university professors, dealing with a variety of new classroom trends, or what I call the flavor of the week. I was very polite and respectful to these collegiate researchers and I enjoyed the coffee and donuts.

But after such educational seminars, I would continue using my successful classroom strategies, techniques, and methods, which catered to the needs of my students.

I have always been a firm believer: "If it works, don't fix it."

The experts, who live in their "ivory towers," have no clue as to what students in local schools need. Likewise, many of these educational theorists have spent little, if any, time ever teaching children in an actual K-12 classroom setting.

Don't misunderstand me. I listened intently when presenters were offering more knowledge in the field of reading. But as soon as they began to tell me how to teach my students, I hit the "off" switch.

• • •

During the winter of 1990, many West Virginia teachers were disgruntled over salaries and there was some talk about a strike while under contract. I informed my fellow teachers at Warwood Junior High School that I would not be walking out if a "Wildcat Strike" occurred. Furthermore, if they wanted to be upset with me, they could start doing so then.

A month later the walkout did take place for a week before West Virginia Governor Gaston Caperton reached a deal with the teachers. I went to school every day that week, verbally assaulted by some "cat calls."

It bothered me none in the least. My teaching philosophy from the very beginning was the "Kids Come First."

Be reminded, my grandfather and mother were teachers. It was their profound belief that promoting student growth was their primary mission. I knew when I chose the educational profession, I wasn't going to get rich.

As for me, my question has always been: "Upon returning to school after a strike, how could a teacher come back in the classroom and say to the students 'You're the most important reason why I teach?'"

Furthermore, teachers always lose the respect of the parents and community-at-large when they strike. I can proudly assert that I never went on strike one single day throughout my entire 40-year teaching tenure. By the way, a few of my teaching colleagues, who did go out on strike, later told me that they regretted being involved with the work stoppage.

Enough said.

• • •

I also have had problems with the missions of various teachers' unions over the years. In West Virginia, there is no collective bargaining (or binding arbitration) in place for state employees. So, public school educators are not required to hold membership in any particular teachers' union.

Still, I joined the Ohio County Education Association (OCEA), the West Virginia Education Association (WVEA), and the National Education Association (NEA).

I had no problem with the local teachers' organization. I was even a building representative in our local teachers' association.

However, I did have some concerns with its state and national counterparts. They went against my beliefs and personal values. After being a member for three years, I decided not to renew my membership.

I am sure many will disagree with my following reasons for dropping out. And I do respect their opinion. I am a conservative by nature, which is contrary to the very liberal beliefs of many in the educational field.

Furthermore, I am strongly opposed to being told by the WVEA and NEA who to vote for in local, state, and national elections; the vast majority of their candidates expounding liberal views.

I have nothing against such individuals except that they don't have the same philosophies and values in life that I do.

I knew that by many I would be called a "scab." I can live with that because personal principles mean much more to me than caving in to others' political agendas.

. . .

Despite my primary desire to focus on the students, my doctoral degree and years of experience opened the door to becoming a leader in the school system. From the fall of 1991 and until the end of the 2000 school year, I assumed the position of "Dean of Students," as well as teaching reading and language arts classes half a day. At first, I was very excited about the challenge of being an administrator, but gradually learned I was most suited to be a classroom teacher. The experience was not very gratifying for me.

As Dean of Students, I was responsible for school-wide discipline, all fundraising activities, and attending various athletic and school functions throughout the year.

I would always jot down a list of "things to do" each day. But I never caught up. Every day brought with it new problems, and the lists kept growing larger and larger day-by-day.

. . .

The hardest circumstances I had to deal with were parents who felt their kids could do no wrong. One mother, in particular, could not accept the fact that her son Shawn was a very unruly student. Every conference I had with her went nowhere.

After I would explain to her Shawn's latest act of defiance, she would simply (and always) say, "Welker, you're picking on my son."

I would likewise respond, "As long as you defend his very poor behavior, Shawn's problems in school will only get worse."

And so they did.

To be honest, Shawn was the worst student I ever had to work with during my 40 years as an educator, including the kids I dealt with in the Pittsburgh Public Schools System. He truly was incorrigible.

Unlike most teenage boys who are mischievous (or irresponsibly playful), Shawn was malicious, mean-spirited, viciously cruel to other students, totally disrespected faculty members, and never felt any remorse whatsoever.

There is some irony to Shawn's story. The summer after he was finished at Warwood, I had to attend a municipal court hearing as a character witness. Passing the hallway that led to juvenile court, I saw Shawn and his mother waiting there to appear before the juvenile judge.

When she and I locked glances, this mother knew exactly what I was thinking: "I told you so."

We did not speak, but she got the message.

•　•　•

I also had to deal with many classroom problems which involved my fellow teachers. Sometimes, they were self-inflicted by the teachers, themselves. On a number of occasions, I had to defend them when I knew in my heart they over-reacted in their classrooms.

I did not like it.

One teacher actually told me that her discipline problems in the classroom were my fault. Why ... because the students had to be so well behaved in my classroom that they came to her class fired up to be disruptive.

Please.

•　•　•

Another teacher, who was a self-proclaimed "master teacher," had the audacity to ask me if I would trade students in my eighth grade language arts classes with her students. She wanted me to trade a couple of my exceptionally-bright students for those in her classroom who were low-achievers and behavior problems.

Believe it or not, I accepted the student-transaction for a number of reasons.

First of all, she didn't like them and they knew it. Secondly, I always enjoyed the calling of working with indifference students and watching them blossom into successful ones. Finally, I treated them fairly: no favorites in my classroom.

Without a doubt, this language arts instructor was a "master teacher," as long as she had brilliant, highly-motivated and well-behaved students.

•　•　•

My Grandpa Bertolette taught me early in life what it takes to be a true educator. He expressed the role of a "master teacher" most eloquently in his book of essays with the following words of inspiration:

A teacher is not measured by the number of bright students he makes brighter, but rather by the number of indifferent students he makes bright. The indifferent child needs the most encouragement.

Many of our greatest men and women were considered dull or slow during their school days. Of course, it takes time and a lot of patience to teach an indifferent student; yet the result may be ample reward.

It is the duty, therefore, of every teacher to know his students, to find out in what they are interested, to associate the uninteresting with the interesting, and in doing so, should appeal to the higher and nobler qualities which serve to move each student.

D. F. Kline Bertolette
Motives in Education
1916

. . .

Another incident I had to deal with was a colleague who swore at a student for misbehaving in class. The teacher would not apologize and the parents were furious. They even considered suing the educator.

In my opinion, all the teacher had to do was request a conference with the parents and principal, apologize, but explain what caused the outburst.

Maybe, just maybe, the parents might have understood, gone home, and reprimanded their child for his behavior in the teacher's class. The situation might have been more easily defused.

. . .

I'm by no means perfect. Over the years, I had my moments of unprofessional behavior as well.

Let me share with you one unbecoming incident where I lost composure. I was on lunch duty and a student was clowning around. I called him an asshole. Immediately after lunch, I went directly to the principal's office and told Mr. Monderine about the profane remark I used to describe this particular student.

Why did I let him know? Well, nobody likes surprises, including school principals. So I wanted him to be prepared for a phone call from the parents, and I would apologize, explaining what the student did.

The principal appreciated me letting him know of my professional transgression. By the way, no phone call ever occurred, but at least my principal was prepared for it.

.   .   .

Oh, I would be remiss if I didn't tell you that I actually received a "death threat" in my capacity as Dean of Students. Our secretary, the wonderful Janet Ackerman, received a phone call where a woman said, "I'm going to kill Dr. Welker," and then hung up.

Naturally, Mrs. Ackerman was beside herself when she reported it to the principal. The death threat was even published in the Wheeling newspaper.

Nothing ever came of it, but it was still a little disconcerting.

.   .   .

After our first faculty meeting before school started for the students one August, a first-year female math teacher said to me that students are always better behaved for male teachers.

I informed her that some of the sternest teachers I encountered as a student were women. One in particular came to mind, Miss Roger, my high school English 12 teacher.

I then began to tell the young teacher about my experiences as a student under Miss Roger's dominion.

There were about 30 of us students in Miss Roger's class, which consisted mostly of athletes – football players and wrestlers.

Miss Roger was very petite in physical stature, being less than five feet tall. To us, she looked as if she was a 100 years old. But her most dominant feature was her eyes. Miss Roger could stare down a grizzly bear, making him whimper in fright.

We were scared to death of Miss Roger. When she taught, you could hear nothing but her bellowing voice.

You never saw so many burly football players and wrestlers cower when she glared at us.

One of her most famous commands was "Don't raise your flags! I will call on you in due time."

We had no choice but to learn in her class, and well we did. Strict classroom discipline is a powerful student-motivator.

A decade later, Miss Roger attended our class reunion. With a twinkle in her eyes, she told us ex-athletes, "I was quite an actress, wasn't I?"

We revered her. As with all outstanding teachers, what was once trepidation morphed into respect for Miss Roger as we matured into adulthood.

Finally, I added, "After establishing control of your classroom, you'll be able to perform wonders with the students."

After the Miss Roger account, I advised the young teacher to do the same right from the start. Be an actress.

Likewise, I shared with her something I was told by a veteran educator, Ed Gaughan, when I first began my teaching career: "Walk into each new classroom like a cross-eyed javelin thrower, and don't smile until after Christmas."

She listened to my advice and today is one of the finest teachers in the school system.

• • •

CHAPTER ELEVEN

The Loss of My Two Iconic Role Models

"Never marvel at the strength of a man's words, but rather by the determination and truthfulness of his actions."
- W. Andrew Welker

Then the bottom dropped out in my life. In the winter of 1998, my father passed away. He had a cardiac arrest. Floyd and I were deeply saddened. We were sincerely blessed. Dad taught us so much in preparing for adult living. He was an iconic individual at home and in his public affairs.

Here's what I wrote about my venerable father in a local newspaper after his passing.

On February 4, 1998, William Howard "Whiskers" Welker told Mother to phone Aunt Jane (his sister), who lived just one block away. Dad quietly explained to Mom that he didn't feel well, and Aunt Jane could help in dressing him for an unscheduled hospital visit.

Dad knew what was happening; his heart was giving out. To the very end, his mind was acutely perceptive. As Mom and Aunt Jane were dressing him, my dad told them "I feel very tired," turned away, and departed from this world at the venerable age of 81.

Later, Mom tearfully lamented that Dad forgot to hug and kiss her before he went. I told her Dad's "hug and kiss" was having her call Aunt Jane, so she wouldn't be alone during his passing.

What a dignified death it was, but it only complimented the life of dignity Dad always lived.

Dad was one of eleven children, whose mother worked diligently as a house-wife, and whose father was a stern coalminer. Grandmother Welker died when Dad was very young, so he never really experienced the devoted love of a mother.

Dad earned his nickname, "Whiskers," as a result of being quite a street-fighter. If you called him "Whiskers" Welker, you were asking for an opportunity to challenge his manhood. From what my uncles have told me, Dad rarely had problems defending his manhood.

He wrestled a little bit in high school, but most of Dad's time was spent shining shoes and working at his father's cigar stores. Grandpa Welker wisely invested his coalmining money in other business ventures. In fact, Granddad owned seven cigar stores when he finally retired from the mines.

As a young man, my father also had to take care of his older brother, Louie, who was crippled by an untimely sports accident. The duties Dad had to perform for my Uncle Louie before he died ... only the strongest of men could understand.

After graduating from high school, Dad opened the doors of his own cigar store, and later, a clothing store, with his "best friend" in life — Andy Ryan. Their very close, almost brotherly, relationship was quite unique for those times. During the 1940s, Protestants and Catholics were deeply divided by their differences in religious beliefs. Dad was a German Presbyterian and Andy was an Irish Roman Catholic.

Go figure.

Then Father fell in love with Dorothy Irene Bertolette, a proper, college-educated girl from the other side of the mining tracks. And she loved him right back with a passion that most people can only imagine. They produced two sons: Floyd and five years later, yours truly.

It was then that Dad and Mom unknowingly humbled the so-called "great ones" in this materialistic, greed-driven world. Dad taught his sons about life and sports, while Mom (along with Grandma Bertolette) instructed them regarding the value of books and the doctrines of Godly living.

Keep in mind, Dad and Mom did everything together as a team. During the joys and sorrows of their 56-year marriage, they kept the family institution strong by their partnership of love.

Now to Dad's lessons in life and athletics that prepared Floyd and me for adult-living. Whatever my brother and I decided to try, Dad was always ready to assist us. Whether it was learning how to ride a bike, hit a baseball, drive a car, carry a football, throw a punch, swing a golf club, shoot a takedown or think for ourselves, Dad was there to guide us.

Dad was also a student of his strict family environment growing up and was not one to accept any excuses in sports or life.

In regards to alibis, I will never forget the night my brother Floyd came home upset after a rough practice in which his coaches were very disappointed with his performance.

It was Floyd's sophomore year in high school. He started complaining to Mom and Dad about how rough practice was and how badly Coach Paul had treated him. As the younger brother, I just sat at the kitchen table and listened.

Mother completely ignored him as she prepared supper while Dad's only remark was, "If you can't take it, Floyd, then quit!"

My brother immediately realized that he would find no pity at home. That night, as the younger brother, I was also taught an important lesson; don't complain to Dad about the extreme physical sacrifices that are part of being a wrestler.

Of course, Floyd stuck it out and it was a very wise decision as you previously learned.

Our most memorable experiences regarding sports involved Dad's nightly wrestling demonstrations on our blanketed living room floor. Floyd and I often practiced with him after our regular workouts at school. Dad had an uncanny understanding of "the basics" in the mat sport.

I smile when I think of two experiences Floyd and I shared with Dad during his after-dinner wrestling workouts.

While still in high school, Floyd broke one of Mom's vases as we were tumbling around. Dad valiantly took the blame, humbly apologizing to Mom, who forgave him ... about a week later.

Then there was the time Floyd came home from Penn State. Dad thought a "new move" Floyd learned from legendary coach, Bill Koll, would not work and he was going to prove his point.

After about 10 seconds of living room wrestling, Dad (who was lying on his back) sheepishly looked up at Floyd and commented, "I guess it will work."

At dual meets and tournaments, Dad never shouted or screamed at us or the referees. Instead, Dad cringed and writhed in the bleachers as though he was the one wrestling. At one dual meet, Dad even fell off the edge of the bleachers in his quiet delirium to help Floyd win. Dad lost the battle with gravity, but his son won, and that was good enough for Dad.

He went far beyond being a loving and totally dedicated sports father. Dad also cared for other parents' offspring, and would never allow us to make excuses if we fell short of defeating our athletic adversaries.

On the contrary, Dad taught us to look within ourselves to determine why our opponents prevailed on the playing field or mat.

As a student, Dad was average in the classroom, but he always admired those who were well educated, especially Grandfather Bertolette. He made it clear to his two sons that higher learning made for a fuller and more well-rounded individual. Dad had the simple, universal wisdom of a contemporary Shakespeare.

Don't get me wrong. Dad was as human as anyone. He was a very opinionated man who had a temper. Dad wasn't one to compromise and could be quite demanding; moreover, he was a stern disciplinarian. But if you understand the times in which he grew up, you would understand the man.

Dad had a very humanistic and compassionate side as well. On a one-to-one basis, he judged people by their actions, not their race, color, or creed. Those people, who had the privilege of knowing Dad, liked and highly respected him.

One intimate note. As a youth, I often watched TV with Dad. Whenever we viewed a sad movie, Dad would cry openly. He was truly a man of abundant character.

Yes, Dad died with dignity, but more importantly, he left his entire family with many, many wonderful memories. The following is my fondest.

When I was about 12 years old, Dad had to admonish me for misbehaving during supper one evening. He didn't spank me. Instead, I received the "quiet treatment" from Dad, which hurt even more. Oh, what I would have given for a spanking.

Sent to bed early, I was extremely depressed and couldn't get to sleep. Dad did not know I was awake when he quietly crept into my bedroom, kissed me on the forehead, and gently whispered "I love you, Billy."

"I love you, too, Dad."

• • •

Fifteen days later, my beloved wrestling coach, Mal Paul, also left his physical body.

Although I wasn't prepared for Dad's passing, I was aware that my legendary coach wasn't well and had a terminal illness.

The previous fall I had closure with Coach Paul. One evening Ron Weller, a fellow wrestler and personal friend (previously mentioned), and I visited him at home. We talked about the many thrills and spills we had on the mats over the years.

Coach Paul then showed us all the wrestling memorabilia he had saved and relished from his mat mentoring days. I was surprised to see the various newspaper clippings and photos he had of me, especially with all the headaches I caused him during my competitive days.

I can still hear him saying, "Well, Billy, which wrestler is here today?"

I was sometimes erratic during dual meets and tournaments. One meet I would convincingly defeat an outstanding wrestler, and, at another competition, I would lose to an average wrestler.

Coach Paul never knew what to expect from me on the mats, and neither did I.

As Ron and I ended our visit with Coach Paul, he gave each of us an affectionate hug. He normally wasn't one to display his emotions. Ron and I were both surprised and pleased by his parting gesture.

That was my final and deeply moving encounter with Coach Paul.

•   •   •

In less than a month, I lost the two men who had the most influence on me during my formative years.

A part of them has always been ingrained in my thoughts and actions throughout life.

•   •   •

CHAPTER TWELVE

A New Era of Administrators: Facing Change Gracefully

"Coming together is the beginning, keeping together is progress, and working together is success."
- Henry Ford

Principal Monderine retired in June of 2000. With the advent of a new administrator in the fall, I resigned as Dean of Students. To be completely honest, I was more than pleased to be back in the classroom full-time. I was quite relieved because any problems I would now have in school were my concerns. No longer would I have to deal with the classroom affairs of other teachers.

In the fall of 2000, Mary Kay Reisinger became the next principal at Warwood Middle School. The school's name was changed when our freshman students were moved to the high school.

Like Mr. Monderine, she was another outstanding administrator who I was looking forward to working with at Warwood.

At first, she thought I was part of the old guard who would resist her innovations. She quickly realized that I was a staunch supporter of her new curriculum and teacher-scheduling ideas, knowing I would do whatever she asked of me.

Since my initial years as a teacher, I have always stood behind all my principals. They were my bosses.

• • •

Although I have always been very cordial with all my teaching colleagues, I rarely went into the teachers' lounge, especially during lunch. I had no desire to listen to petty concerns that were counterproductive to a positive school environment.

About this time, we became very high-tech in our educational setting. When the white boards were installed in our classrooms, we were given instructions on their various uses as a classroom teaching tool.

It's truly ironic; I started my teaching career with a black board and ended my career with a white board.

By the way, I also had my very own "tech team." Whenever I was having difficulties operating the white board, I would call upon one of my own "tech team" members, a sixth grader, to show me what to do.

I was pretty "tech savvy."

• • •

Unfortunately, not everyone was as tech savvy as me. I received an unbecoming e-mail from one of my students during the early 2000s. I must admit, it was pretty raunchy, with inflammatory remarks about my species.

The student concluded the e-mail with the following statement, and I quote: "Dr. Welker, I'm one of your eighth grade students and you'll never find out who I am."

Being a great detective, I solved the problem about a second later. On the top of the e-mail was HIS NAME. Well, at first I thought, "No, he can't be that stupid. Probably one of his buddies got on his computer."

Nope. We learned from his mom that he was the instigator.

When the principal suspended the boy for a couple of days, I actually felt sorry for the adolescent.

Although his mother was so humiliated by his action, I tried to comfort her by explaining that her son was a good student in class and we got along great. He just did something stupid.

Maybe I was reminded of some of the acts of stupidity I performed during my teenage years.

Anyway, I sincerely felt sorry for him and his mom.

•   •   •

At this point, I must make a teaching confession. My practices in the classroom environment have always been a bit unconventional.

Although I ran a tight ship in the classroom, I did possess some compassion for the students. Whenever I saw two kids fighting outside my classroom door, I quickly escorted them into my room and closed the door. Standard school procedure required me to take them to the principal's office where they would be immediately suspended for three days.

Instead, I would give them a lecture, explaining the severity of their actions. I made them shake hands and informed them that I would not hesitate to send them to the office if it ever happened again.

Very grateful, none of them ever fought in school thereafter.

•   •   •

My test-taking philosophy was also quite unorthodox. I handled "cheating" as a learning lesson. Instead of giving the student an "F" for the evaluation, I would enter no grade for that test.

I would then tell the offender, "Look, as much time as you took to cheat on the test, you probably would have passed the quiz without copying the answers from your cheat sheet" (or whatever inventive technique they devised).

The least one can say about students who cheat on tests, they cared enough about their grades to do so. Some students, who have absolutely no parental support for succeeding in school, don't even put out the effort to cheat. They just don't care.

Yes, I would cut first-time offenders a break with the caveat that the next time they attempted to cheat, they would indeed receive an "F."

•   •   •

Why did I have such an indulgent teaching practice regarding the act of cheating? Well, when cheating in my classroom occurred, I was reminded of my senior year in high school in World Cultures class.

Our teacher was Mr. Mal Paul (yes, my wrestling coach). My grade for most of the year was around a "C+."

The day of our final examination, I was sitting behind John Matichak, a whiz in the course. Surprisingly, I received a 99 on the final test. Mr. Paul was more than impressed; he was quite suspicious regarding my grade on the final exam.

He asked me point blank, "Billy, did you cheat on the final exam?"

"Mr. Paul, I just studied really hard for the test. I wanted you to be proud of me."

"Yeah."

Decades later when I was inducted into our regional sports hall of fame, my wife Peggy and I were sitting with Mr. Paul and Mr. Weaver at the social gathering after the ceremony.

I said to Mr. Paul, "I have something that has been bothering my conscious for years. Do you remember the final exam I took in your history class my senior year?"

"Of course I do; I accused you of cheating."

"Well, I'm going to be honest with you now. Mr. Paul, John Matichak cheated off me."

"You little son of a bitch," he said with a smile.

• • •

I didn't just show compassion to students who screwed up, either. There is one heartwarming classroom incident I will never forget. My eighth grade class was reading Jack London's *Call of the Wild*. The entire story was about a dog named "Buck." While I was reading a part in the book where Buck was being beaten, I noticed one of my female students was crying.

I walked up to her desk and asked, "Ashley, what's wrong? Does Buck's beating bother you? Remember, it's only a story."

"It's not that, Dr. Welker. As you were reading, it got me thinking about my dog that died yesterday. He was our family pet for 15 years."

I hugged her.

• • •

With the advent of "political correctness" during my final years as a teacher (which I define as "avoiding the truth"), Principal Reisinger had to tell me that I could no longer say "Shut Up" to my students. She informed me of this matter outside my classroom.

At the same time, some students were talking in my class. So I slowly turned around, looked them straight in the eye and shouted "Shut Down!"

Ms. Reisinger smiled at me and walked away, mumbling under her breath, "You're a piece of work, Dr. Welker."

I thought, "Yep, I get that a lot."

•   •   •

In the fall of 2005, Principal Reisinger transferred to another school in the county. My next principal was Woody Yoder, who was the former art teacher at our school. He was a very compassionate and superb school administrator.

Principal Yoder was only with us for one year, but during that time he made some innovative adjustments in all of the school's content areas. In doing so, Warwood was named a National Blue Ribbon School of Excellence by the U. S. Department of Education.

One of Principal Yoder's novel approaches was the creation of a reading tutoring period for students who were below mastery on the state competency test. I was charged with developing the reading strategies to be incorporated into the remedial reading program.

I was given a two-hour time slot during the school day to work with 20 students who were in dire need of such personal instruction on an individualized basis. I worked with one student per half an hour. That fall they were all reading at the "partial mastery" or lower level.

I spent the entire school year preparing them for the reading competency tests in May. My basic instructional method was to utilize various forms of test items and develop mini-lessons from them, teaching such reading skills as main ideas, context clues, levels of comprehension, figurative language, etc. It was a microcosm of one of the approaches I utilized in my regular developmental reading classes for years.

To further validate the value of this reading strategy, the International Reading Association actually published the approach in one of its publications: *The Journal of Reading.*

At the completion of the reading sessions, I felt confident that all my students had improved their reading skills. The year-end state competency evaluation in reading would ultimately determine the success of the program.

In June, Principal Yoder received reading results and called me into his office. I must say I was most definitely apprehensive regarding the outcome of my teaching practices to improve my students' reading skills.

"Dr. Welker, I have just read over the reading scores of your 20 students. Last fall, they were all reading below the mastery level. Well, today, 85-percent of them are reading at the mastery level. Great job, Bill!"

"Next year, Mr. Yoder, we'll shoot for a 100-percent!"

Well, that never happened.

After Mr. Yoder left to assume an elementary principal's position in another school system, it was determined by the central office administrators that our one-on-one reading program was too time consuming for such few students. Thus, the remedial reading program at Warwood was dropped.

In the end, the dollar was more important than the student. Sadly, I have witnessed such administrative practices far too many times as a classroom teacher. I have always been amused by the hypocrisy of some powers to be when they profess that student learning is the number one priority regarding their educational decisions.

• • •

CHAPTER THIRTEEN

Our Family's Plight and Help from High Places

"You must get involved to have an impact."
- John H. Holcomb

When our youngest son, Dan-E., graduated from Wheeling Park High School, he basically spent the next year partying with his friends. But that lifestyle changed abruptly one morning when he woke up with a huge hangover after a night of carousing. Dan-E. finally came to the realization that his life was going nowhere.

He informed Peggy and me that he decided to join the U.S. Army, and did so the very next day. We supported his decision. It has always been my contention that if a high school graduate has absolutely no idea regarding his future, joining the armed services is a wise choice. Our son made the right decision.

• • •

On one of Sgt. Daniel E. Welker's visits home, he met a young Filipino girl, Mary Jo Decena, who had been working at a local Wheeling restaurant. About two years later, Daniel and Mary Jo were married while he was stationed at Fort Drum in New York. Shanen, the younger of our son's two stepdaughters, witnessed the ceremony. Like her mother, she had a United States visa at the time.

Though it was a very special occasion for them, Daniel and Mary Jo also wanted to reunite with his older step-daughter, Aaliyah. She was still in the Philippines with her grandmother.

Since the early 2000s, Dan and Mary Jo had been trying to acquire a visa for Aaliyah, but have been stonewalled by every governmental agency they have contacted.

They were becoming more and more frustrated with a process that should not have been so difficult, especially for an active U. S. Army sergeant. In the meantime, Mary Jo studied diligently and acquired her United States citizenship. They also had a new addition to the family, Vander, a baby boy, prior to Dan's assignment to Iraq.

Upon returning from over a year of deployment in Iraq in 2004, Dan and his family were reassigned to a tour of duty in Germany. They were able to obtain German visas for Aaliyah and her grandmother, Violetta, to live with them.

That summer, Peggy actually flew to Germany to visit the young Welker clan, meeting Aaliyah for the first time. In the fall of 2005, they again applied for a United States visa for Aaliyah at the state department in Frankfurt. Dan and Mary Jo were still getting nowhere.

It was then that they asked Peggy if she and I would try to contact politicians at home to plead for Aaliyah's visa.

That's when the family matriarch, Peggy, kicked it into high gear, telling me that we were on a diplomatic mission to get our step-granddaughter the visa she so much deserved. Peggy first tried to contact the United States Citizenship and Immigration Service and was placed on a long hold. When she finally did speak to an agent, Peggy was informed that Dan and Mary Jo must call them – a grandmother had no say.

Dead End.

Her next course of action was to contact our congressman Alan Mollohan, as well as West Virginia's U. S. Senators – Robert Byrd and Jay Rockefeller. It was not an easy assignment. We were given the run around by Congressman Mollohan's office, being told they would get back to us. They never did. We were given the same treatment from Senator Byrd's staff.

We did receive some satisfaction from Senator Rockefeller's office. One of his staffers, Wes Holden, investigated the matter, but even he was having difficulties locating someone in authority that could help us.

Peggy even called the U.S. Embassy in Frankfurt, Germany from our home in Wheeling to find out why her son and his wife were having problems with a visa for Aaliyah. The person on the other side of the line was very condescending and rude, finally hanging up on her. Being part Irish, Peggy was furious, and being of German descent with a temper, I, too, had the same sentiments regarding our diplomats on foreign soil.

Throughout the entire process, Peggy and I also began to feel the same emotional frustration that Dan and his family have gone through for a number of years.

It was amazing to us that thousands of illegal aliens (a lot of them criminals) are crossing the southern border of the United States, many ultimately receiving visas, while our son, who's fighting for this country, is hitting one bureaucratic brick wall after another.

It just didn't make any sense whatsoever; lady justice was truly blind regarding the government's complete disregard for the simple request by one of its own combatants.

After a dreary fall with no results and the Christmas season quickly approaching, we were at a loss as what to do. Still, we continued writing letters and calling anybody and everybody we could think of who might be able to help.

We received some bittersweet news after the holidays. Dan would be completing his duties in Germany by spring and his family would be visiting us during Easter, minus Aaliyah and Violetta.

Not good.

The other negative news, Dan would be heading back to Iraq for another tour of duty that summer, leaving his family behind again.

We still had our problem. But then, an opportunity presented itself.

We learned that President George W. Bush was actually going to visit Wheeling for one of his town hall meetings in March. Of course, Peggy and I thought maybe, just maybe, we could somehow make President Bush aware of the visa dilemma that one in his military was experiencing. We couldn't help but feel it was our last avenue of hope for Aaliyah.

Then Peggy said to me: "Why don't we contact the paper?"

Fortunately, I had strong connections with the local newspaper, having penned a weekly Sunday sports column on wrestling during the mat season, which I initiated in the late 1970s. Furthermore, I was a close friend of the newspaper's editor, Mike Myer, who I had worked with for over two decades on other public-interest stories and politically-oriented columns as well.

At first, we didn't really have a plan of action, so we needed to get all our ducks in a row before I called Mr. Myer. It was then that Peggy further suggested that I author a "Letter to the Editor" and have it published the day of President Bush's arrival, praying that the President or one of his staffers would read it and take action.

Now note: When national politicians speak in areas outside the "DC Beltway," they most definitely want to know about any problems a particular area is experiencing so they are ready to answer questions that may come their way. Simply stated, they want to be prepared to deal with the social concerns of that region.

I told Peggy the letter to the editor was a great idea, and I actually called Mike Myer at home on a Sunday evening. I told him of Dan's and Mary Jo's problem and what we wanted to do.

After explaining our son's predicament and what we wanted from the paper, the editor said: "No."

I was shocked: "What!"

"Let me finish, Bill," he continued. "This is too big of a story to handle as a letter to the editor. This is front page news."

"Great! So where do we go from here?"

"Well, tomorrow's Monday and President Bush is coming on Wednesday. Will you and Peg be home at 7 p.m. tomorrow?"

"Absolutely."

"I have a young, ambitious investigative reporter who I want to interview you and Peggy. That will give him a day to research the matter further and put together a potent article for the Wednesday paper. We'll run it right next to the President's arrival article in the morning so he will learn of your son's struggle to get your step-granddaughter's visa. Hopefully, the President will be prompted to assist one of his soldiers."

"Mike, that sounds like an outstanding idea."

When I finished my call with Mike Myer, Peggy and I began to prepare for Monday's interview. We wanted to make sure that the reporter understood completely all that Dan and Mary Jo went through in their heartrending quest to procure a visa for Aaliyah.

Monday evening Peggy and I welcomed Adam Townsend into our house and began to tell him all the facts that led up to this final course of action and public outreach on Aaliyah's behalf.

We sat in the living room drinking Cokes, as Peggy and I continued telling Mr. Townsend what had transpired for years, dealing with the red tape of government bureaucracy. Peggy and I spilled our guts out explaining to Adam this unfair drama in our democratic society.

I actually broke down when I showed the reporter a crystal cube of glass which depicted a frosted holographic image inside it, displaying three-dimensional portraits of Aayilah, Shanen, and Vander with a banner underneath that stated: "We love you Grandma and Papa Guy."

Again, my emotional side of OCD was kicking in as I felt the sadness that Aayilah must have been experiencing during this period in her life.

Then Peggy asserted, "I know we have all these governmental laws and regulations for everything under the sun, but for our son being a soldier, you would think they would expedite the visa process for his step-daughter and our step-granddaughter. Not so."

She further contended, "As a regular American citizen, I promised Dan that I would contact any federal agency I thought could help. I got nowhere. So now I'm at my wits end. Our final hope is that we can make the President take notice when he comes to town this week."

Adam Townsend took our story to heart. He promised that he would put his total investigative-writing skills in gear to make our family's saga of frustration known to the general public – and the POTUS.

Townsend did an excellent job writing a lengthy, compelling article emphasizing how long the Welker family has been in a diplomatic struggle with the United States Citizenship and Immigration Service (CIS).

He wrote, "It has been a long and frustrating journey for the Welker family. Suffice it to say, the Welkers worry that their son, Sgt. Daniel E. Welker, will be deployed to Iraq before the visa is approved. The CIS is thinking in terms of months before approving the visa for Aaliyah."

The news story concluded with one final plea from Peggy, "It's very obvious why we are telling Aaliyah's story now. We are hoping that President Bush hears about this problem and intervenes with the CIS."

President Bush's town hall meeting was to be held at Wheeling's Capitol Music Hall. The powers-to-be at the newspaper informed us that they could reserve us front-row seats for the event to give us more visibility regarding our family's fight for Aaliyah's visa.

Peggy and I decided against it. We didn't want to come across as protesting the government or the President. Our only concern, or should I say hope, was that President Bush would become aware of our family situation and come to our aid.

Both Peggy and I were at work while the President's town hall meeting was taking place.

That Wednesday afternoon Peggy started to receive phone calls from Congressman Mollohan's, Senator Byrd's and Senator Rockefeller's Offices regarding our story in the newspaper. They were tripping all over each other to finally come to our aid. It was then that we realized the power of the press. But it gets even better.

Adam Townsend received a phone call from Emilio T. Gonzalez, Director of the United States Citizenship and Immigration Service. Mr. Gonzalez told Townsend that he would do everything in his power to help expedite the process for Aaliyah's visa.

Director Gonzalez fulfilled his promise. That Friday night, after federal office hours, Mr. Gonzalez called Peggy (somehow he acquired her phone number) and told her that visas for Aaliyah and grandmother, Violetta, were ready at the U. S. Embassy in Frankfurt, Germany. (I wonder if the individual who hung up on Peggy had to perform the honors.) Gonzalez further informed Peggy that they could pick up their visas that Saturday when the embassy is usually closed for diplomatic business.

We were elated!

On Saturday, Dan and his entire family drove to Frankfurt. They were greeted with the utmost respect and were quickly escorted to the appropriate office where they received their long-awaited visas.

It's unfortunate that an American soldier had to go to such lengths of petitioning the highest official of the land to get results. Still, Peggy and I truly appreciated President George W. Bush and his staff for intervening on Aaliyah's behalf.

In the end, the Executive Branch of the United States Government saw to it that a soldier under the President's charge was given the due consideration he and his fellow peers rightfully deserved.

In reality, it's totally unconscionable that a member of the military had to go to such extremes to get results in a few days that previously took years to accomplish, going through the proper channels that did nothing, or even cared.

That's governmental bureaucracy at its very worst. No American citizen, be it civilian or military member, should ever have to be treated as though their legitimate situations are insignificant and worth no action from civil servants who chose not to help. Shame on them.

As for the Welker family's plight, Peggy and I couldn't thank President Bush enough in a letter we sent to him a week after Dan and his family's visa requests finally reached fruition.

• • •

On April 12th, the entire Welker family was reunited at my daughter Tiffany's house in Wheeling. It was a great homecoming for Dan, Mary Jo, Shanen, Aaliyah, grandma Violetta, and baby Vander.

Even neighbors were outside shouting, "You got her." It was a very special Easter weekend for us. But it was also a bittersweet experience since Sgt. Dan Welker received his marching orders for Iraq in June.

In all, Dan actually spent three tours of duty in Iraq, which we felt was a bit much to be placed in harm's way. On the other hand, that's part of being a soldier.

The good news, except for Iraq, Dan's family has always been able to be with him wherever else he was stationed.

As Peggy and I look back at our son's and his family's visa ordeal, we feel so indebted to Mike Myer, the newspaper's editor, and especially Adam Townsend for his outstanding reporting; he really did his homework.

The Welker family lauds his efforts on our behalf. We weren't alone. The West Virginia state newspaper association honored Mr. Townsend with a top award as an "Investigative Reporter" that year.

Sometimes you can fight city hall – and win.

• • •

CHAPTER FOURTEEN

The Final Years: Enjoying the End of My Career

"Take your work seriously, but yourself lightly."
                              - George Bernard Shaw

As my teaching career approached its finale, I relaxed more and more into my sense of humor and love for students.

My last principal in the fall of 2006 was Andy Garber, an outstanding educator I have known for many years. Like me, he had a devious sense of humor.

I once invited him to observe my class when I was reading the short story, *An Occurrence at Owl Creek Bridge*, by Ambrose Bierce. The short-story title was viewed on the white board.

The setting of the narrative takes place in a southern state during the American Civil War.

After reading the tale, I always asked 10 questions and one "extra credit" query: "What very famous body of water flows under the Owl Creek Bridge? Now remember, students, this story takes place in the South during our tragic American Civil War."

Invariably, the vast majority of my students would answer, "The Mississippi."

Principal Garber then shouted, "Owl Creek, you fools; it's written on the white board!"

"Ah, Dr. Welker, that's unfair; you tricked us!"

I then simply said to them, "Look, students, if you have any complaints about my teaching, set up an appointment with my secretary, Helen Waite. Just go to Helen Waite!"

Before leaving the room, Principal Garber leaned over my desk and whispered, "Doc, you're a piece of work."

•   •   •

One short story we read in my classes explained how many animals were transported to America from other countries.

When they learned that bulls were shipped from Spain, I couldn't help myself. I went on to inform them that such crew members were known as "Bull-Shippers."

"Students, there are still Bull-Shippers working today. If you meet one, I want you to be aware that Bull-Shippers tend to exaggerate and embellish when telling their very descriptive yarns. Be smart; don't listen to their Bull-Ship stories."

It was amusing to see the smiles on some of my students' faces.

•   •   •

On numerous occasions over the years, I had to digress from the classroom lesson a bit. I noticed that during lunch recess outside on the playground, many of my middle-school boys did not know how to wear baseball caps. So, I saw the need to orchestrate a demonstration on how to wear a baseball cap.

Using my own cap, I asked the class, "What is this long-curved flat thing protruding from the front of the baseball cap?"

They responded, "It's the bill."

"Very good. Now for a little tougher question. What is the purpose of the baseball cap's bill?"

"It's to keep the sun out of your eyes."

"Well, there you go…and let me demonstrate with my cap. Boys, when you're wearing your caps with the bill in the back, like this, you're defeating its purpose and the sun blinds your eyes."

They always began to laugh.

"Some of you are getting the idea when you turn the bill of your cap to the side, like this. All you need to do at this point is to grab the bill and slide it to the front, like this. There you have it. Your eyes are protected from the sun."

After the lesson, it would always take me awhile to quiet the uproar in my classes.

It seems my seminar on baseball caps failed, as one can continue to plainly see.

• • •

I guess I wasn't always a very inspiring teacher in the classroom. Why do I say this? Well, on occasion a student would fall asleep during my class. I had a solution for that.

Since we didn't have bells in the school, I would gesture to the rest of my students to be silent.

When the period was over, they tiptoed out of the classroom. I would then have the next class sneak quietly into the room to their seats, carefully seeing to it they did not wake the napping student.

When the student finally woke up, he was shock to see the faces of students other than his classmates.

As the rest of the students began to laugh, the expression on the sleepy student's countenance was priceless.

• • •

Speaking of rest, as I neared my retirement, I still went to school early, but only because Peggy had to be at the dental office at 6:30 in the morning to set up for the day's patients.

After dropping her off, I traveled on to school, an hour and a half before the students entered for daily classes.

I was no longer a morning person, so I had a pillow and blanket in my classroom, along with an alarm clock. I laid down on the blanket, as my head sank into the pillow, and went back to sleep until five minutes before school started.

Time takes its toll on us as it passes by. That early morning catnap was refreshing. It prepared me to deal with my young fledglings with the same enthusiasm as I did at old Edgington Lane Elementary School, now a neighborhood playground.

•   •   •

I had about a millions ways to make lessons more fun. I authored an unpublished short story, *One-In-A-Thousand Odds*, which I shared with my older eighth grade students.

It was about a dedicated junior high school math teacher, John Langston, who learned that his petite wife, Jane, was having an affair. He partially blamed himself because he was so engrossed with his students and their progress, paying little attention to her wants and needs.

When he learned who the other party was, he was furious because he considered his wife's lover, Bob Turner, to be a good friend from college. John tutored Turner in many courses. If it wasn't for him, Bob would never have graduated.

In John's mind, the only alternative was to kill Bob Turner in defense of Jane's honor. John meticulously plans the murder, using all his knowledge regarding mathematical outcomes. To him, the plan was foolproof and the odds of getting caught were one in a thousand.

But as fate would have it, John was not aware of one very significant detail, and was arrested just hours after the crime.

Ironically, it was a former student of Langston, Detective Dave Forsyth, who arrested him stating, "I hate to arrest you, Mr. Langston, because I always respected you as a teacher. Had it not been for that hidden camera, the odds of solving the murder would have been one in a thousand."

Langston replied, "How true."

"Mr Langston, you have the right to remain silent …"

My students have always been intrigued with the tale. But I'll never forget one student's question regarding my writing.

"Dr. Welker, my parents tell me you publish articles in the newspaper on various topics. Where did you learn how to write?"

"Well, Suzy, when I was a senior in high school, I was going steady with a girl one year older than me who found a job in a city about 60 miles away.

"She stayed there during the week and came home on weekends. I wrote her love letters every day. So I wouldn't be repeating myself, you know, using the same words over and over again, I referred to my thesaurus to aid me in expressing my affection for her with various vocabulary endearments. Guess what happened, Suzy?"

"You married her, Dr. Welker."

"Hell no, Suzy! She dumped me and married someone else. I wasn't even invited to the wedding."

The whole class busted out laughing.

. . .

In the summer of 2008, I determined it was time to retire at the end of the school year. It would be my 40th year as an educator. Had I worked another year, I would have lost money. I'm not the sharpest tool in the shed, but I was able to figure that one out.

. . .

I must admit, my last year teaching started off quite surprisingly. An unexpected challenge was about to come my way.

One week before football season started that summer, Principal Garber phoned me and asked if I could meet him at the school. I had no idea what he wanted.

At first, I thought he might have wanted me to be his assistant principal my final year at the school. I had an administrative certificate and no one had yet been named for that position.

Mr. Garber immediately cut right to the chase, "Bill, I need you to coach football."

Totally dumbfounded by the request, I explained to him I hadn't coached football for nearly twenty years. Furthermore, I was more of the "paperwork guy" back then for the 7th and 8th grade team. I really had no say in teaching and drilling plays because we had four coaches: two for 7th and 8th grade and two for the freshman squad. Furthermore, in those coaching days, Warwood Junior High School was not known for producing winning football teams, and I was part of that legacy.

"Look, Mr. Garber, I can't coach football. I was the assistant coach under Coach Bill Donohew. I can't even remember winning a game. Haven't you ever heard of the 'Wrong-Way Turner' affair? It's legendary in Warwood. We had just scored a touchdown and were down six points with a minute and a half left in the game. Jeff Turner was the kicker."

"Jeff Turner, our maintenance supervisor?"

"Yes. We told him to kick an on-side kick. All our boys were lined up to the right of Jeff. When the referee blew the whistle, Jeff kicked a perfect on-side kick to the LEFT. Their player picked it up and easily ran for a touchdown with no Warwood 'Viking' defender in front of him. Coach Donohew and I tried to hide behind each other; we were so embarrassed. No, Andy, you do not want me coaching football."

Having finished giving every excuse I could think of, including my age, Principal Garber finally said, "BILL, I NEED YOU TO COACH FOOTBALL."

How could I say no?

Now note: There were only two football coaches at the school my final year since all the freshman students were sent to the high school when we became a middle school. So, my responsibility was to prepare the 7th grade football team for games. In other words, I had to put together the offense, defense, and special teams, and mold them into a functioning athletic unit on the field.

The bottom line: I had to actually coach a sport in which I had practically no background experience or knowledge.

• • •

As previously mentioned, my only experience as a football player was in 7th and 8th grade, and that was back in the late 1950s. Moreover, I was a third string defensive "nose guard." I played over 90% of my football on the bench, getting in the game (on rare occasions) when the score was 40 to nothing, either way. Point being, I was clueless when it came to coaching the "gridiron" sport.

• • •

Now back to August of 2008. My savior was Head Coach John Chacalos, a meticulous student of the game who was in charge of the 8th grade team. He knew he had his hands full with me right from the get go.

For example, Coach Chacalos suggested that I move two of my seventh graders to the flanker and tailback positions during the first week of football practice.

My response was "Sure, coach. Now, where are those positions?"

But I learned; Coach Chacalos was also a great teacher. And I got smart; I decided to fall back on strategies that worked for me as a wrestler and mat sport coach.

The four key elements I utilized with my football players were: discipline, drill work (on every offensive, defensive, and special team play), conditioning, and organization.

It worked!

To make a long story short, we entered our final seventh-grade contest of the season with a .500 record, and it was a home game. We were leading at halftime, but our opponent tied it up 20-20 with minutes left to play in the fourth quarter.

Now here's where I truly demonstrated my football expertise.

With only three minutes left in the game, I felt a slight tug on my coaching shirt. It was a football player's father, who was working the chains. He politely mentioned, "Ya know, Coach Welker, you get three time-outs per half in football. This might be a good time to start using them; don't ya think?"

After explaining that there are no timeouts in wrestling, I gratefully thanked him and took his advice.

I called my final timeout with 15 seconds left in the game. We had possession of the ball in midfield, a long way from the goal line. But with a couple of football games under my coaching-belt, I knew exactly what I was going to say to the quarterback.

I finally asserted my football-coaching prowess by saying to him, "Grove, what do you think?"

"Coach Welker, I think the 9-0-2 pass play will work."

"Go for it!"

I must admit, though not being Roman Catholic, I believe I crossed myself and said a few "Hail, Marys" as the ball took flight. On the receiving end was one of our two outstanding flankers, Eric, who caught the ball and ran in for the touch down with only 10 seconds remaining on the clock.

Then I decided to attempt a two-point conversion. The boy who ran in the plays asked, "Coach, what play should I give Grove?"

"You tell Grove to call whatever the hell he wants."

Grove's play-choice worked. We won the game 28-20, ending with a winning season and my boys were ecstatic.

The last thing I remember was looking back toward our field house and seeing Coach Chacalos smiling, while shaking his head in awe.

Some of my overly zealous players had asked me to coach again the next year, following my retirement from teaching. But after that final "last-second" home game win as a football coach, which allowed me to leave the gridiron sport in style, I had to say:

"Thanks, guys, for your confidence in me, but you deserve someone who is far more knowledgeable in the game of football than I am."

They compassionately disagreed and each of them gave me a hug. I was touched and had to turn away before they saw my eyes moisten.

•   •   •

My final year in the classroom was a wonderful experience. Things that would have upset me with my students for the first 39 years, I basically ignored. Yes, I had mellowed.

•   •   •

All the students knew it was my last year. On morning duty, as the students walked through the front doors, I would greet them with a friendly, "Welcome to Walmart," and gave them happy face stickers.

•   •   •

I knew I made the right decision to retire one Friday afternoon in the winter of that year. Every Friday, we had SSR, an abbreviation for "Sustained Silent Reading." During this time, the students had the opportunity to read whatever appropriate material they enjoyed. As the classroom role model, I would also silently read.

It was about two o'clock during a Friday SSR session when I dozed off for a second while reading. When I opened my eyes, there was nobody in the classroom.

I was in a state of confusion when I heard laughter. It came from the hallway. As I looked that way, I saw my students and Principal Garber pointing their fingers at me, shouting, "Gotcha!"

Payback's a bitch.

•   •   •

That spring, Mr. Garber coaxed me into coaching track. I was in charge of the distance runners, both boys and girls. One of my milers was Zach. In our first two competitions, he easily won his event.

Zach also played baseball and missed about two weeks of track practice. We allowed the kids to play both sports. When he returned, Zach lost to his closest competitor hands down.

It was at that point that I came up with a strategy.

"Zach, we have four weeks before the league's track and field championships. Forget that loss, you just have to get back into running shape again, and we have plenty of time."

"Coach, I'll beat him in the next meet."

"No you won't."

"Why not? Don't you think I can beat him?"

"No. I just want him to get comfortable. In the next three events, I want you to trail him by about 15 yards, and let him win. We're going to lull him to sleep."

"What do you mean? I can beat him"

"I know you can, and you will in the league championships. Here's the plan. You will again trail him by 15 yards until you reach the curve for the final stretch. At that point, you will sprint to the finish line. He won't have time to react."

Zach won by 50 yards, clinching the team title for my boys.

· · ·

It was a fun year and I decided go out with some flare. At the end of each year we always have a school "talent show." I shocked my principal and colleagues when they saw me on stage singing "The Titanic," accompanied by all my eighth grade students. It was a hoot.

· · ·

My final day of classes with the students was emotional for all of us. At the conclusion of each period, I hugged my students. Some even had tears in their eyes. I, too, was having problems holding them back.

With the completion of my 40-year teaching journey, it dawned on me. Of my 62 years on Earth, I spent 57 of them in a classroom in one capacity or another.

· · ·

The afternoon of the final day for teachers I sat at my desk in front of an empty classroom. Thinking of the days when I was a student, I realized that not being a perfect adolescent made me a more effective teacher. I knew all the tricks and often told my students, "You can't snow the snowman."

During my teaching career, I made a heck of a lot of mistakes in the classroom. On the other hand, I always tried to help those countless, defenseless students who struggled in class and didn't believe in themselves.

They were my innocent sparrows over the years; the ones who worked so hard to please me and fit in with the rest of their classmates. They had the warmest hearts and wanted to sincerely succeed in their lives. Like those heroic athletes I witnessed throughout life, who received no glory during their school days, these students possessed a spirit that wouldn't quit. Remember, not everyone is destined to be an eagle.

One such student of mine was quite shy. I did my utmost to make him feel important because he tried so hard in my classroom.

His work ethic paid off. For the last 20 years, he has been a dedicated and very responsible water-works employee for the city.

He is most definitely a productive citizen in our society. That is something that millions of other individuals in American can not claim.

•   •   •

I then thought about my encounter with the principal earlier in the day. I remembered saying to him, "Ya know, Andy. As I think about all my classroom pranks, my less than sterling scholastic grades, and being vertically challenged, I have to say that half my students were more mature than me, the other half were smarter than me – and all of them were taller than me!"

He was amused.

"All kidding aside, you're forgetting a couple of important points, Bill. All the students respect and love you … quite a teaching legacy. I will miss your compassion for teaching and your positive and humorous view on life."

"Do you honestly respect me?"

"Without question."

"Then why do you think that during my four decades of teaching, I never had a student teacher?"

"Bill, come on."

With a smile he continued, "We didn't want you screwin' up the minds of aspiring teachers. You do have some strange classroom strategies that only a teacher with your personality could get away with. How about the times I've seen you lecturing to the students standing on top of your teacher's desk?"

"It gets their complete attention."

"Dr. Welker, there's nobody that can motivate students like you have done for many years. But you have to admit you're way out there when it comes to teaching methodology."

"Okay, I guess that answers my question. Hey, after school let's go to Abbey's for a couple 'brewskies.' I owe you one for putting up with me."

"You're on."

• • •

Near the end of the day, I looked at the sign in the back of my room. As I read it: "Excuses are like sewers, every street has one and they all stink," I began to reminisce.

Fairness was the keystone regarding my relationships with all the students. I then remembered what an eighth grade boy once jokingly said to me, "Dr. Welker, you don't like me."

"That's not true, Bobby. I'm not prejudice; I don't like anybody."

He smiled.

Firmness was the foundation of my discipline practices in the classroom. Likewise, I was reminded of what another outspoken student told me, "Dr. Welker, you're a mean little man."

I thanked her for the compliment.

She laughed.

I guess that's what I enjoyed the most about being a teacher, seeing my students "laugh," especially those who rarely did. It always reminded me of a quote I once read by A. G. Ingersoll: "One laugh of a child will make the holiest day more sacred still."

• • •

Well, it was time to perform my final act as a teacher, recording student grades, before walking out of my classroom for the last time.

I began to average their grades, but then suddenly stopped.

My concluding thoughts as an educator were: "Oh, the hell with it. Every one of my students gave it their very best effort all year long."

So, in my professional opinion, they all deserved and received "A's" the last nine-week grading period.

I felt inspired.

After everything I have said and done in my life, I guess they were all right. I was, and I still am: "A Piece of Work."

• • •

EPILOGUE

Although this is a story about me: the boy I was and the man I became, it is also a story of my mother and her prayers. Looking back, I've seen how her prayers have protected and led me through my many self-induced mistakes to prosper.

On June 4, 2011, that wonderful woman, who accompanied Billy to the principal's office so long ago, began a new eternal life with her Father in heaven. Mother's spiritual foundation was built around her deep devotion to the Trinity — God the Father, God the Son, and God the Holy Spirit.

By her example, Floyd and I not only learned how to pray, but even more importantly, we learned the power of prayer in our lives.

As our protector, whenever Floyd and I got into trouble with Dad, she would calm him down and save us from dire consequences. She even went as far as to tell Dad little "white lies" to save our young hides. I'm sure Dad knew. However, due to his steadfast love for Mom, he let some of our childhood transgressions pass.

After Mom's funeral, I began to feel guilty for not always being the best of sons. I thought of my losing patience with her as Mom got older. I wanted to tell her one last time, "I'm sorry, Mom, for all I put you through growing up, for sometimes being moody, and for not telling you how much 'I love you' more often."

I was so saddened by these thoughts while cleaning out the house that evening. After disposing of some old clothing in the trash can, I happened to see a glint on the sidewalk from the street light.

When I picked it up, I was amazed to see it was a lapel pin in the shape of a heart with a dove connected. Even after her departure, Mother sent her unconditional love filled with forgiveness. I wear it to this very day.

Thanks, again, Mom.